Man Sharing

DILEMMA OR CHOICE

Man Sharing

DILEMMA OR CHOICE

A Radical New Way of Relating to the Man in Your Life

Audrey B. Chapman

KAYODE PUBLICATIONS LTD.
15 West 24th Street
New York, N.Y. 10010

None of the persons mentioned in the case studies are based upon my professional caseload. Much of the material was gleaned from the many and various participants in man-sharing workshops that I have conducted around the country. All the names used are fictitious and some are composites of several people. No personal information was used, however, without the individual's consent.

Library of Congress Cataloging-in-Publication Data

Chapman, Audrey B.
Man sharing : dilemma or choice.

Bibliography: p.
1. Polygamy—United States. 2. Adultery—United States. 3. Interpersonal relations. I. Title.
HQ981.C47 1986 306.8'423'0973 86-8486
ISBN 0-688-04455-7

Printed in the United States of America

1 2 3 4 5 6 7 8 9 10

Kayode's 1st Printing June 1991

Acknowledgments

This book is dedicated to my mother, Alice Lee Chapman, who has made an enormous impression on my life through her tremendous love, strength, and encouragement. Throughout my life her message to me has always been the way to survive as a female, that is, through self-love, healthy dependency, and ability to take calculated risks. She also reminded me that a woman can be anything she wants to be; and when things fail you have the sole responsibility for changing them.

I will always be indebted to this gracious woman.

This book could not have been written without the support and encouragement of Judith Simpson, who assisted in

ACKNOWLEDGMENTS

the writing and research of the manuscript. A special thanks goes to her daughter, Mia, who was so patient on the many evenings we worked late into the night. I would also like to acknowledge Dr. Carolyn R. Payton, Jo Katherine Page, Reginald Nettles, William Mayo, Alan Hermesch, and Henry Duvall. Appreciation also goes to Pat Goldblitz, editor, and Jennifer Williams, editorial assistant, for their tremendous guidance and support during many painful stages in the manuscript.

Thanks to Roslyn Targ, my literary agent, who never wavered in her faith in me and the material. She often kept me from feeling hopeless and supplied spiritual energy for me to move on.

Special appreciation to Joy Shelton for the tremendous time and energy she provided in the form of moral support and typing services. Also thanks to the various clerical support staff who assisted in typing. And to the many women across the country, friends and associates who willingly shared their stories with me. Finally, I must gratefully acknowledge the continual support of my family—without them this effort would have been most difficult.

Contents

CONTENTS

Contents

Comes the Dawn

After a while you learn the subtle difference
between holding a hand and chaining a soul,
and you learn that love doesn't mean leaning
and company doesn't mean security,
and you begin to learn that kisses aren't contracts

and presents aren't promises,
and you begin to accept your defeats
with your head and your eyes open,
with the grace of a woman, not the grief of a child,

and learn to build all your roads
on today because tomorrow's ground
is too uncertain for plans, and futures have
a way of falling down in mid-flight.
After a while you learn that even sunshine
burns if you get too much.
So you plant your own garden and decorate
your own soul, instead of waiting
for someone to bring you flowers.
And you learn that you really can endure
that you really are strong
and you really do have worth
and you learn and learn . . .
with every good-bye you learn.

—Veronica A. Shoffstall
New York City

Introduction

While waiting for a train in New York's Grand Central Station recently, I found myself staring uneasily at the ceiling and thinking I had had the experience before. There was something familiar about the antique lighting and glazed marble tiles lining the walls; even the wooden bench on which I sat had a hardness I seemed to recall. As I searched my memory for clues and tried to reset the scene, it hit me. I had sat in that very spot seven years before, weeping as I had contemplated a divorce from my, then, husband.

We had come down to New York from New Haven, Connecticut, to celebrate our tenth wedding anniversary with dinner and a Broadway play. Later, while waiting for a return train to New Haven, we sat in a cozy restaurant, sipping cocktails and discussing the appropriately titled play *Don't Bother Me, I Can't Cope.*

I mentioned one section of the play in which some of the female characters had discussed the pain they experienced in dealing with some men. Pointing out that the actresses presented a pretty one-sided view of male-female relations, my husband said, "Men aren't always to blame. Sometimes the way a woman deals with her man drives him into the arms of another woman."

Of course, I agreed and told him so. But then he went on to say, "I believe it's possible for a man to find a woman who's sensitive, caring, and in tune with her man's needs." At that point I felt uneasy and told him it didn't sound as if he were generalizing but talking about a particular woman. As I held my breath, he told me, in fact, he was.

He had been having an affair with one of his coworkers for the previous six months. Although I had suspected it, I had kept my suspicions to myself. As he tried to explain what she gave him that I didn't, I told him, "Don't bother. I know. She's young, talented, and exciting." Shrugging his shoulders, he nodded and said, "Yes." Then I asked him the big question: "Are you in love with her?" Looking away momentarily, he nodded again, yes.

From that moment on I lost touch with reality; I stood and barely heard him call my name. It seemed as if everything upon which I had based my very existence—even the floor beneath my feet—had disappeared. I became a space traveler and blindly groped for the door. Then I was outside, finding my way up Broadway and onto Forty-second Street.

The next thing I knew I was on Fifth Avenue, and there on the corner I confronted the very thing I had tried to escape in the restaurant: my own rage. I let out a shriek and began screaming while people moved away or asked, "Is anything wrong?"

Everything was wrong! And as the light changed a hand touched me; I saw my husband and sanity returned. I sobbed and wailed as he led me to Grand Central Station, saying, "You must collect yourself. It's not as bad as you think. We have a lot to talk about."

Back at the station, he left me momentarily, and I sat on the same bench on which I was to sit years later, except then I contemplated doing something I had never done before—living alone. Two months later, my husband and I were separated; within a year, we were divorced.

During that period, my sister and a number of female friends and colleagues experienced separations and divorces. Each of us questioned her womanhood, trying to answer the question "How did I lose my man?" But there were no answers. One night, at a dinner party that could have been described best as a hen session, we cautiously talked about our dissolved marriages and some of the problems we faced with our men. To everyone's chagrin, one of the facts that emerged that evening was that we had all suspected that we had been sharing our husbands with other women—in some cases, for periods up to a couple of years.

Although some of us vented our bitterness, a few of us tried to take stock of the situation. We concluded that the problem lay in society, in the subtly secret and different ways we were raised as boys and girls. "Be chaste and preserve thy virginity for thy husband," we had been told, while boys had heard a message in different tones: "Get all you can get and enjoy it." Perhaps once it had been appropriate for society to send out different messages—before so many women had taken advantage of opportunities to develop their careers. But now, perhaps the price I had had to pay for my professional degree and career was to be without a man, or worse, I mused, to share another woman's.

I resolved not to share another woman's man. But later, when I moved to Washington, D.C. (where the ratio of men to women was once alleged to be about one to seven), I saw women condemned to man sharing and aggressively competing for males who, overestimating their value, refused to make any commitments.

In my work as a human-relations trainer and counselor I conduct many women's support groups, where I hear horror stories from women who are actively man sharing. Although the focus of these workshops is on male-female relations, the group discussions constantly shift to the question "How can I find a good man who is monogamous?"

Like any professional trainer or counselor, I offer my own opinion sparingly. In the beginning, I felt I had to tell most of the women in these groups that I didn't approve of man sharing. In response, I heard things like, "Wake up. Sometimes if you don't share another woman's man, you don't have any," or "Most of us are sharing anyway. What difference does it make?" The brutal honesty of these women made me stop and think. I began to ask myself if men really were naturally promiscuous and women more inclined to being dependent and monogamous.

I had always pitied women in cultures in which men were allowed to have more than one wife and be with as many women as they liked and could afford. Suddenly, I realized that those women had a decided advantage over women in my own culture. They had rules and understood the game they were forced to play. However, while I didn't find their established modes of docility and deferment to their men particularly attractive, I had to admit that those women could never be shocked or hurt by their men the way I or my girl friends could by ours. Of course, they suffered. But unlike so many American women, they didn't sit home at night watching the clock and wondering where their men were.

Eventually, I realized that if our society, driven as it is by technological upheavals, is going to continue on a course bordering on polygamy, then American women need a set of guidelines or rules to ensure their emotional and sexual survival. It became clear that man sharing is a reality that can no longer be ignored.

During the spring of 1983, I held my first workshop, "Man Sharing: Dilemma or Choice." Although I expected only 50 women to attend (a number slightly above the usual attendance for such workshops), 110 women showed up. Most of them, if not all, had been or were involved in some form of man sharing. My goal was to help these women with their feelings of helplessness and being oppressed in their relationships with men. The task was to enable them to better cope with man sharing.

Introduction

The women came for a variety of reasons: Some women were involved with married men; others were in relationships with single men who would make no commitments; and still others were recently separated or divorced and were trying to put their lives back together. There was even a seventy-year-old widow present who told the group, "This kind of forum could not have occurred when I was young." She had come to get some answers for her daughter, granddaughter, and some female friends. All, according to her, were involved in some form of man sharing.

The man-sharing seminars I conduct in Washington and elsewhere have been comprised of women of all ages, ethnic groups, and professions. As one woman said, "Each time I developed what I thought was a monogamous relationship, I discovered another woman in the picture." Perhaps more frightening, another woman confessed that she had given up the quest to find a man and had been celibate for several years. Yet another woman said she had found a more realistic way to deal with male promiscuity: She accepted it and played the game herself. "What's good for the gander can be better for the goose," she said.

Several of these women, as well as a handful of my colleagues, friends, and associates, urged me to write a book about man sharing, saying that it was something that could no longer be swept under the rug. Further, they felt that if women do it, it deserved a name. While I believe that everything, no matter how unpleasant, deserves to be identified or named, I do not think that naming things so that we can have a neatly labeled world serves any purpose.

I decided to write this book to ease the suffering and to cut down on the anger, guilt, and pain experienced by so many women who are man sharing or contemplating doing so. I prefer to believe that it was for these reasons that I embarked on this venture. While I still do not advocate man sharing as a permanent way of life, I believe man sharing is a social condition in which some people feel they have no choice but to be involved—for a variety of social and psychological reasons.

As I point out in the chapters that follow, man sharing of some sort probably will be experienced by most women at some point in their lives. However, man sharing is not for every woman. While some women may consider sharing a real choice, some will never accept this awful reality. It is my firm belief that women shouldn't concentrate on the shortage of men as the source of all their troubles. The following pages will introduce coherent strategies for turning what seems like a bleak situation into what can be a real opportunity for women to creatively pursue individual growth and development—with a man or without one.

MAN SHARING
DILEMMA OR CHOICE

CHAPTER 1

What Is Man Sharing?

Sharing has been defined as cheating or playing around.
Whatever you feel, it still suggests confusion, conflict,
and curiosity for most, whether you participate or not.
—ANONYMOUS

WHY SOME WOMEN RESIST— WHY SOME DON'T

What is man sharing? When I used the term in May 1983 at my first workshop on the subject, some people expressed rage and others disappointment that I would dare to discuss publicly the reality of infidelity in relationships. They made me feel that I had single-handedly designed this society where nonexclusivity is the norm, not the exception.

People are puzzled when I say that sharing affects most of us at some stage in our personal development. Then I point out that there are four basic types of sharing situations: single woman/single man, either of whom sees others; single woman/married man; married woman/single man; and married woman/married man. With these numerous possibilities comes a great deal of mischief.

No one will openly admit that sharing is desirable, but statistics indicate that American men and women have been engaged in the practice for many years. Still, my openness about sharing makes many uncomfortable. Many men feel that they have a personal stake in keeping the reality of this situation away from women. They feel women are much more compliant when unarmed with the truth.

There are women who also want sharing kept in the closet, because once it's out, they must deal with it. Women are socially reared to believe that monogamy is the only way for them to function in relationships. Having always received the subtle message that it's "bad" or immoral for them not to remain exclusive in relationships, many women feel they can't consciously accept sharing. They feel better holding on to their fantasies about men and romance, even though these delusions tend to set them up for unhappiness.

It is clear that, for many reasons, sharing is not a pleasant subject, but it is one I feel women must face openly if they are to approach their personal lives with some semblance of sanity. Let's face it, no one, including myself, wants to share a loved one with someone else. However, like it or not, many of us are participating in shared relationships that bring us much turmoil and confusion. Armed with a better sense of reality and some basic information, I believe that women can open their eyes and decide to take better care of themselves in relationships.

There is a shortage of available men in this country (the facts of which will be discussed in the next chapter), and some people have used this shortage as an excuse to leap into some new styles of relating. Married men readily offer themselves to women who want intimacy for just a night, and married women, feeling insecure about the stability of their own marriages, go out to explore new terrain. And singles have begun an endless round of social gyrations, passed off as relationships, that reflect the growing insecurity about what it means to be involved in an exclusive relationship.

The lack of commitment between men and women is a popular subject today, and an atmosphere of declining commitment is very conducive to sharing. The more people you can get yourself involved with socially, the less involved intimately you will be with any one of them. The same is true with sexuality. If you have many partners, you tend not to care very much about any one of them. The so-called sexual revolution has made it possible for all of us to have as many sexual partners as we can manage, but many women aren't coping very well with their newfound freedom. In many instances, they feel that men have used sexual freedom against them by deciding to take no responsibility in sexual relationships. So, many women who participate in obviously shared situations do so with great internal conflicts. They hang in there because they fear being without a man, yet they devote much of their psychic energy to trying to change him and somehow force him to make a commitment to monogamy.

But there is a small group of women who have decided they no longer have the energy to fight reality, and they are opting for shared relationships that they create on their own terms. I like to call this group women of choice. They have made a choice to control their own personal lives, regardless of what men do or don't do, and regardless of what society thinks.

Confusion and frustration, however, are experienced by both women of choice and by those who resist. The women opposed to sharing feel powerless because they are surrounded by a reality they refuse to accept. The women who don't mind sharing often feel some ambivalence about how to best bring it off when no guidelines really exist for women who choose nonexclusive relationships. Thus, even women of choice are struggling to make sharing work in an environment not wholly compatible with nonexclusivity for women.

Women of choice are unquestionably in the minority; most of the women I talk with in my travels are desperately trying to hold onto monogamy as an ideal. However, these women are at a great disadvantage sexually. The woman who cherishes the monogamous ideal feels she can't enjoy sexual fulfillment unless a man tells her that she's his one and only. There was a time when a man would say, "I love you," and promise to stay forever just for the sake of taking a woman to bed, but few men today feel so inclined. Men are much more open about having other women in their lives, and that leaves the monogamous woman in a quandary.

Women of choice are in no such quandary, because they don't expect men to commit to them just for sex. They seem to enjoy their own sexuality to the point that commitment is of little concern to them if they find a man physically appealing. They may surround themselves with several men to ensure that they always have a sexual outlet. If one man becomes unavailable, for whatever reason, they always have another.

Some women say that if women accept sharing and opt to participate, they ultimately become no different from the irresponsible men women complain about so much. This is probably true for women who accept sharing as a permanent life-style. But the women who seem to handle it best, and seem the most well-adjusted emotionally, are those women who share only at certain times in their lives. These women remain open to a more intimate relationship with a man if the possibility of one presents itself.

WHY SOME PEOPLE DON'T HAVE A CHOICE

A group of people, both male and female, exists who are compelled toward nonexclusive relationships because they need the emotional reinforcement that being involved with many others can bring. For some men and women, one mate will never be enough—their narcissistic personalities require constant gratification. These people tend to mistrust the loyalty of others, so they multiply their partners for protection. They also tend not to want to be alone; they thrive on attention and receive individual validation based on the numbers of people they can win to their hearts.

Individuals who fear abandonment are often chronic sharers. They might have had a parent who died, who was emotionally distant, or left them as a child. They may also have experienced great trauma after a divorce or death of a spouse. Not wanting to ever feel this sense of loss again, these people surround themselves with many adoring men or women. These are not always conscious reasons, but often remain in the subconscious. If an individual never confronts these hidden fears, he or she may be propelled from one shared relationship to another for a lifetime.

There is yet another group of people who share and do not have a choice. They are the men and women who lacked wholesome love-object relations that were constant and consistent during their early childhoods. They may have been dealt with in hostile, demeaning ways or overindulged with attention. They experience both positive and negative images of themselves. This phenomenon is known as "splitting"; it interferes with the integration of self-concepts.

Later on in adulthood, these individuals find it difficult to love without emotionally "splitting." They are unable to integrate love objects in a wholistic manner. So affairs, whether married or single, become a way of continuing to "split" love objects into "good or bad."

I believe that the failure to form healthy attachments in childhood is a major reason why some people are comfortable only in shared situations. For example, some of the men and women I have interviewed mention that they had a domineering mother or father, a subtly seductive parent, or a smothering parent. Because of these parental problems, a child might feel unable to bond with either parent. Ultimately, this child may suffer some feelings of emotional deprivation, or the child may become an adult who perceives love as controlling or engulfing.

Howard Halpren, in his book *Cutting Loose: An Adult Guide on Coming to Terms with Your Parents,* writes that people who constantly seek to win someone who belongs to another are replicating the Oedipal wish of childhood. The little girl or boy who yearns for the parent of the opposite sex all to himself or herself will often grow up searching for a man or a woman who is unavailable on a permanent basis.

I have had women come to me who cannot figure out why they always find themselves in relationships with married men, or men who have commitments to other women. Some of these women stay in these relationships for years, hoping that eventually they will be able to win this unavailable person. They never realize, however, that if the person they desire were to become free, they would probably flee and find someone else who is unavailable.

Consider Betsy, a forty-seven-year-old single physician who

lives in a rural area in the West. She met a married man whose company she enjoyed, but who told her from the start that he wanted to preserve his marriage. He said he cared for both Betsy and his wife, and if Betsy could accept this, they could have a wonderful time together. Betsy never really had had any long-term relationships. After her relationship with the married man went on for many months, she decided to try to win him away from his wife. Tension soon developed between Betsy and her lover, but she couldn't give up her fight. Fearing that she was losing her battle to win this man from his wife, Betsy came to me anxious about the prospects of being alone again.

After exploring a number of issues with Betsy, I discovered that her father had been a workaholic whose erratic behavior had made uncertainty the foundation of her formative years. She desperately wanted her father's attention, but she was never able to get it and hold it because his emotions were never constant.

Men can exhibit similar behavior in adulthood. Maxwell, a thirty-three-year-old electrician, described to me a life that fits the playboy stereotype. He's attractive, soft-spoken, and quick with the words of passion. He sees many women and says he enjoys his social life a great deal. One day, he met a woman he thought was different from the others in his life and soon began to feel attached to her. She, however, wasn't interested in being part of a harem, so he had to make some decisions about his other women. Although he wanted this "special" lady, he didn't feel able to let go of all the others. He said that something inside of him wouldn't allow him to feel safe in an exclusive relationship, not even with someone he loved. "It's too risky," he said many times.

Maxwell is the oldest of four children who grew up in a matriarchal family. He was very attached to his mother, who loved her children but ruled the household with a firm, domineering hand. Since her relationship with her husband was a cold, purely functional one, she was able to form excessively close bonds with her children, especially her son Maxwell. He loved his mother, but felt controlled by her. He said he had had similar feelings of being controlled on those rare occasions when he thought he was in love. Sharing, thus, became a comfortable life-style for this man, because he never had to deal with the anxiety of being controlled by any woman.

From time to time, people like Betsy and Maxwell will feel some conflict about the choices they make in their social relationships, and they may seek to change these familiar patterns. Then, of course, there are other people with backgrounds similar to Betsy's and Maxwell's who choose sharing as a way of life and who have no desire to change a life-style that seems to feel right to them.

SHARING AS A CHOICE

Since sharing is not going to go away, I advise women to keep their options open. Sharing is not for every woman, but every woman needs to open her eyes so that she can recognize when she is sharing her man with someone else. Moreover, each woman needs to decide whether or not she can handle a shared relationship. Too many women pretend that they can share in order to have a relationship and then end up overwrought with anxiety. Having a man certainly isn't worth all of that, even though I readily admit that having a man who genuinely cares for you is worth a great deal. What having a man is worth is something each woman must learn for herself. Every man in a woman's life need not be a potential mate, but any man a woman relates to should provide some of what the woman feels is important to her emotional well-being.

What Is Man Sharing?

My theory is that women who are comfortable with sharing as a choice are those women who feel the need to master their environment. They usually have spent years learning to control their own behavior so that their lives move in a direction they desire. They are reluctant to let someone, especially a man, have any control over them, so decision making in a relationship comes very easy to them. In fact, some men might find these women a little too aggressive for their tastes, because women of choice generally do only what they want to do in a relationship. When, or if, things go awry, they tend to blame neither the men nor themselves. They go into a relationship with few expectations of permanence or of becoming dependent on the man of the moment. They call themselves realists, even though to most women their life-styles would be considered extreme or offbeat. They allow little time in their lives for depression, which makes them always refreshing, since many women, especially those who come to me, are depressed and feel victimized by a society they don't understand.

CHAPTER 2
Lonely Statistics

There are women who swear the numbers were fabricated and perpetuated by men bent on manipulating the odds in their favor.

—BEBE MOORE CAMPBELL

When my marriage ended and I finished sorting through the emotional debris, I faced yet another problem—what to do with the rest of my life. I had always wanted and planned for a career, but like most women, home and family were to be the centerpiece. It was just a matter of time, I thought, before a suitable mate would show up.

I had long ago given up the dream of knights in shining armor. My girl friends, who had been single longer than I, had learned to do things together and saw men pretty much as inscrutable creatures who needed women for "only one thing." I, however, determined not to spend a lifetime of sharing, planned to have male companionship—and eventually to find a real man who would commit himself only to me. I believed there were plenty of men out there; certainly they all hadn't packed it in and gone home. Time passed and no line of lonely bachelors queued up at my door. The wait, however, was worth it, because I made a discovery—a sad one but a real one. There really is a surplus on the distaff side, and any way you look at the columns, the numbers don't add up.

It is hard to overcome a lifetime of conditioning, but overcome some women may have to do. Not all women are going to have mates, not even if every available man were willing to commit himself. I demonstrate this fact in my man-sharing workshops by telling the women that if each of them stood up and asked for one man all to herself, one quarter would be left standing—as if in the adult version of musical chairs. There simply are not enough men in America to go around, and the reasons for this situation are complex, varying according to age, ethnic group, social class, and geographic location.

According to the United States Census Bureau, in 1980, there were 116,473,000 women compared with 110,032,000 men, a difference of slightly under 6.5 million females. In the central cities of the metropolitan areas, the ratio was 90.8 males per 100 females, but in rural areas, men slightly outnumbered women 100.1 to 100. There were slightly fewer than 30 million unmarried women in the United States compared to 21.5 million single men. Of course, these numbers vary depending upon the age group you fall into and which statistics you happen to review.

We may get better as we get older, but the disparity in the sex ratio worsens with age. If you are between 30 and 34 years old, there are 102 women per 100 men. But there are 128 women for every 100 men in the 35 to 39 age group. If you are between 40 and 44, women outnumber men 135 to 100. Statistics also suggest that among the divorced, especially within the 30 to 44 age range, there is a 42 percent surplus of women.

In *Too Many Women? The Sex Ratio Question* by Marcia Guttentag and Paul F. Secord, the question of a "marriage squeeze" is explained by two facts—women tend to marry men a few years older than themselves and the birth rate is declining. According to William Novak in *The Great American Man Shortage and Other Roadblocks to Romance: And What to Do About It,* the situation is particularly acute for women born in the 1940's, who are now in their mid-thirties. For example, a woman born in 1947, looking for a man a couple of years older than herself, faces a rather grim situation, since in 1945, almost a million fewer babies were born than in 1947. Additionally, these "older" men are generally already married, thus further tightening the pool of available men. The gay rights movement also influences the number of available men, because homosexual men no longer feel they have to get married in order to be in step with the larger heterosexual population.

However, sheer numbers are just part of the story. Other factors combine to make the game of romance roulette a real game of chance.

In *Too Many Women?,* Guttentag and Secord raise the hope that the numbers *might* balance out by 1990, but a balanced national picture will still leave certain groups of women without potential partners. Black women between the ages of twenty-nine and forty-two will still outnumber available black men three to two in 1990. The younger the black woman, the better her chances of finding a mate. The authors note that at least thirty out of every one hundred black women are squeezed out of the marital pool with no potential opportunities for mating.

It is also estimated that by 1990 there will be about 116

to 118 men for every 100 white women from twenty-three to twenty-eight years of age. While women reaching the age of thirty-three or older will continue to experience better marital opportunities than black women through the 1990's.

Numbers! Numbers! Numbers! We can belabor the statistics, which portend lonely existences for many American women, and debate their significance for endless hours, but the question comes down not to raw numbers, but to the number of *available* men in any particular category.

Another reason there may appear to be a male shortage is the manner in which some women choose their partners. Some have such high expectations for their men that it's not surprising that they complain about the limited pool of available men. I have been unable to find definitive data to fully outline the reasons for the male shortage. Whatever they are, the shortage leaves many women with the awful reality of sharing and competing for those few men who are available.

The imbalance in the sex ratio gives the male more freedom of choice and sense of control in his relations with women. But why should this be so? Women must learn to participate in decisions of relationships or men will continue to dictate romantic situations that suit their own needs. Because we feel overwhelmed by "the numbers," women fall into the trap of thinking that men can do pretty much whatever they want. We live in a social milieu very conducive to sharing men. Overt and covert polygamous relationships will continue to thrive as long as society continues to wink at the existence of such relationships. Even a cursory look at today's dating games will prove that some Americans speak of monogamy, but, in fact, don't practice it.

SHARING EASIER TODAY THAN EVER

During the past ten to fifteen years, American society has undergone a number of social changes that have created an environment that breeds shared relationships. We lived through the "me" decade, where self-gratification was exalted above nurturing and caring for others. And we are still trying to cope with the shifting roles of men and women, and the differing expectations that have accompanied these shifts.

A significant problem between men and women today has to do with the fear of being too close, which produces anxiety. Much of this anxiety is a direct fallout from the sexual revolution, when both marrieds and singles got on a fast track away from intimacy and one-on-one relationships. With the need to avoid closeness came fear and an impulse to escape. What better escape than sharing? Sharing keeps emotional attachments at a minimum and makes demands on either the male's or female's part unrealistic. You can't ask for anything because the other person might run from you into the arms of another. In my experience, there seems to be an escalating tension between men and women that gets played out in various ways that often no one understands: Women exert enormous energy trying to maneuver men into traditional styles of relating, and men are frustrated and confused by traditional women in "modern woman" disguise.

Today's social order has become murky with ambiguity, and many of us are still uncomfortable as we struggle to let go of the past and deal with the reality of the present. But while some of us are struggling, a small number of others are feeling that quasi-polygamous relationships might be the answer to all this groping for a new way.

Lonely Statistics

There was a time when the ultimate fantasy, especially for men, was the freedom to have multiple sexual partners without the strictures of guilt and responsibility. The women's movement made it possible for women to catch up with men in the fantasy game, so they, too, began to think of having more than one sexual partner. A move toward sexual freedom and a more relaxed moral code resulted. The ultimate fantasy was now possible, but few people seemed to be having much fun. Discos, singles clubs, and computer dating became the accepted way to meet and make a brief connection. Sharing became even more of a reality because married men and women were involved. As a way to avoid intimacy, sharing became a viable option.

One of the many reasons for sharing is that it creates a way to keep romantic attachments diffused. And diffusion, of course, is at the root of some sharing games. We live in an era of "declining commitments," not just to people but to many traditions that were dear in the past. Alvin Toffler, in his book *Future Shock,* explains the loss of commitment this way: "As we rush toward super-industrialism, we find people adopting and discarding life-styles at a rate that would have staggered the members of any previous generation. For the life-style itself has become the throwaway item." He goes on to say that when people have no real commitment to or consensus on a life-style, they obviously have no loyalties to a committed relationship. Explaining that people have come to expect relationships of short duration, they protect themselves by not becoming overly involved. Therefore, when the end comes, they are cushioned from the hurt. But, of course, while everyone is posturing for fear of getting hurt, real intimacy is never given a chance to develop.

Sex has become a public commodity; it is often used as a game of keeping score, and recent surveys show that women are catching up in the game of who can have the most notches on the belt. *Cosmopolitan* magazine surveyed single women to determine how many lovers the average woman has had in her lifetime: about nine was the average. Typically, most women had had two to five, but a sizable 15 percent of the respondents had had more than twenty men as lovers. There were even some who had had thirty men by the time they were out of their teens.

Sexual promiscuity has become a real issue for both men and women, especially because of the increased awareness and concern over certain sexually transmitted diseases, especially AIDS (acquired immune deficiency syndrome). People ask me if this disease will stop sharing from taking place. The answer is a resounding no. You may see men and women significantly cutting down on the numbers of people with whom they are sexually involved, but human nature, being what it is, says that even a killer disease won't stop people from getting around monogamy. For example, a married man may limit himself to just one other woman whom he feels is a reasonably safe risk. But no one said that sharing has to be about great numbers of people. If more than two people are in a relationship, sharing is taking place.

CHAPTER 3

Sharing: Old Game, New Twist

Those who can and want to live their lives monogamously should do so; but those who cannot, those whom it will destroy, should have the possibility of making other arrangements. After all, the establishment of a "new life" is predicated on recognizing the contradictions in the old one.

—WILHELM REICH

POLYGAMY IN OTHER CULTURES

Toqua Jameel Muhammed is happily married but has been thinking lately that perhaps the time has come for him to take a second wife. He has discussed this prospect with his current wife, who has no strong objections to a cowife as long as she helps choose the other woman who will occupy her home. Muhammed has thought long about how he wants his household to work, and he thinks eventually he will require four wives—two to work with him in running the family business and two whose main task will be maintaining the household. A devout Muslim who works as a medical technician, Muhammed's interest in setting up a polygamous household is deeply rooted in his religious beliefs; he emphatically denies that it has anything at all to do with any erotic fantasies on his part. However, Muhammed is not from a Far Eastern or African country where polygamy is an accepted life-style. He is American-born and -bred, and he intends to set up his polygamous household of four wives and their children right here on American soil.

For women living today in Muslim Nigeria, their religion, which allows a man to take as many as four wives, still influences their life and relationships. However, according to a 1984 article in the *Washington Post,* some women are struggling to find a means of self-fulfillment, even though their religion requires that "respectable" women remain in seclusion in the same household with cowives who don't always embrace each other in sisterly love. Author Beverly B. Mack, who spent three years studying the lives of Hausa Muslim women in Kano, Nigeria, writes that by feminist standards in America, these women, through a system of seclusion and polygamy, might seem reduced to a life of slavery. "But a Hausa woman growing up in her culture understands the demands made upon her and is prepared to deal with them on her own terms," Mack observes.

When I listened to Toqua Jameel revel in the glories of polygamy and read about women like those in Kano, Nigeria, I wondered how many Americans have ever considered the numbers of people in this world who make polygamy a permanent life-style. If we are honest with ourselves, we can search our backgrounds and uncover "sharing" situations that, to be sure, were not sanctioned by law, but persisted as viable relationships nonetheless. Who hasn't heard stories about previously unknown children appearing at the death of a male family member. A lawyer told me of an experience he had while growing up in the South. It was common knowledge, he said, that his father had another family "down the road," but that no one talked about it. His father apparently earned enough money to keep both fami-

lies in necessities, and the lawyer can't recall seeing or hearing his mother in dismay over the situation. At the time of
his father's death, both families showed up at the funeral—
one sat on one side of the church and the other family took
the opposite side.

The irony in this and in similar situations is that sometimes these women and their children are not necessarily a
surprise to the wife. She may have known about a second
family for some time and chose to ignore it in order to
preserve her own family unit. These surreptitious quasi-
polygamous relationships represent what I call polygamy
American-style. In countries where polygamy carries religious and legal sanctions, men and women know what they
are getting into, so surprise is not a factor, as it sometimes
is in the United States.

"Polygamy is a common practice still in certain regions of
the world," according to researcher Nsenga Warfield Cop-
pock. "What you find is with the advent of Christianity and
a Westernized way of thinking people will do less of it and
more young people will rebel against it. But there will always be a group of people who will continue to practice it.
Statistics show that eighty-seven percent of traditional African societies continue the practice of polygamy."

Polygamy, a term generally defined as the practice of having more than one spouse, is as old as civilization itself. The
tradition has been in place in some cultures for so many
years that, even now when Western values threaten to en-
croach upon some of these more traditional societies, it is
not without much conflict. The practice of a man taking more
than one wife came about for various reasons, the least of
which, according to most scholars, was sex. In ancient societies where farming and tending the land were the chief
means of making a living, polygamy became an important
part of an overall economic system in which a man needed

many hands to keep his livelihood going. Polygamy has an agrarian basis, but it is also part of many of the world's major religions.

The religious and economic aspects of the practice of having multiple wives is generally overlooked by some Westerners, who tend to view marital relations with purely sexual and romantic overtones. This is not the case in many Eastern and African countries, where many times marriage has nothing to do with our notion of "being in love." Instead, the practical advantage of having free farm labor by having many family members outweighs any sexual or romantic needs. However, it is true that Western values have strongly influenced many world cultures, and polygamy has been outlawed in some places, such as in China and Turkey.

In India, where polygamy was once practiced on a wide scale, now it is no longer permissible legally. However, because Indian society is made up of people of diverse religions—Hindu, Muslim, Christian—the laws governing marriage follow religious doctrine. Dr. Thomas Wessel, a practicing psychologist who grew up in a southern region of India, described the role of the concubine, or mistress, in the orthodox Hindu community. Whereas a wife is traditionally the mother of the children and keeper of the household, he said, the concubine is desired for sexual pleasures— she even may come from a lower caste than the wife. At one time, Wessel said, concubines were known as the "Temple Dancers." They were the property of the temple, where they lived and danced on ceremonial occasions. In certain religious sects, part of the temple-dancing ceremony called for the devotees to have sex with the dancers. In this way, a concubine could make a living, often becoming the mistress of some rich man.

Wessel reminisced about how insulated he was from these delicate matters as a child until one day, shortly after finishing college, he began talking with a friend, who was about nineteen at the time.

"For a long time I didn't know too much about his family background," Dr. Wessel said, remembering his old friend. "He talked some about his father visiting him in his home, and I wondered and finally asked where his father lived. He then told me that his father lived on the other side of town. To show how naïve I was, I then asked why his father didn't live where he lived. My friend had about seven siblings, and they all lived together with their mother. His father was from an upper caste—a Brahmin—and he and his mother were from a lower caste, because his mother was this man's concubine. He came to see the family of his concubine almost every day, and since it was a small town, the other family was no secret. Of course, the two families were kept clearly separate. For example, if his father was entertaining or celebrating some important holiday, the concubine's family wouldn't be included. Another interesting aspect to this particular situation was that my friend said that whenever his father came to visit them, he wouldn't eat in their house, because a man from an upper caste couldn't eat in the home of members of a lower caste.

"This really blew my mind," Dr. Wessel said with a smile. "He could sleep there with this woman, but he couldn't eat there."

The economics of the situation were also perplexing, Wessel pointed out. The primary family, of course, lived very well, in keeping with their high station in life. The family of his friend, however, did not live nearly so well. They had to ask for money for the necessities of life. In the past, there were laws to protect the concubine and her family; now, however, the laws do not provide for these kinds of situations. Women clearly did better when laws existed to protect their rights in polygamous situations. Wessel said that

41

although polygamy was outlawed in India when the country became independent, old traditions die hard, and even today men who want more than one wife find loopholes in the law so that they can take multiple spouses.

Sometimes the wife would even "assist" her husband in taking a concubine, if she was unable to bear him any offspring. When asked why any woman would agree to this arrangement, Wessel observed that Indian women are brought up to believe that one of their primary functions in life is to please a man. "Even though we have many professional women—doctors, lawyers, etc., even our prime minister, who was female—they still are taught the importance of catering to the male."

Mythology says much about what is valued in a particular culture, and it is very difficult to undo centuries of indoctrination. Wessel illustrated the Indian woman's devotion to her husband's needs by using a Hindu myth. As the story goes, "This woman carried her ailing husband on her shoulders up into the hills to a prostitute's home so that he could satisfy his sexual desires."

Once a divinity student, Dr. Wessel believes that it is generally difficult for Americans to see the religious implications of the practice of polygamy. Americans too quickly judge cultural practices they don't understand in moralistic tones, which never allow for a real grasp of the mores of the culture in question. Toqua Jameel also lamented the fact that many of his Christian friends "gave him the blues about polygamy and how wrong it is, but I always ask them have they read their Bibles closely. Abraham had a wife, Sarah, and another woman, Hagar, and a number of the prophets had more than one wife."

In addition to Abraham, a number of Old Testament figures took concubines. Among these men were Jacob, Gideon, David, and, of course, King Solomon, who had seven hundred wives, princesses, and three hundred concubines.

The Old Testament prophet Isaiah did not speak kindly of sharing women, even though polygamy was practiced in his day. In the fourth chapter of Isaiah it is written, "And in that day seven women shall take hold of one man, saying, 'We will eat our own bread, and wear our own apparel, only let us be called by thy name; to take away our reproach.' " Isaiah was warning the Hebrew women of the consequences of what he saw then as a frivolous life.

Cultures in which polygamy is practiced generally accept it because more women are available for marriage than men. Assistant Professor Leachim Semaj of Cornell University has stated that a historical analysis shows polygamy has thrived in cultures where a wide discrepancy exists between the numbers of available men to women. As we have already discussed, in America males are and have been greatly outnumbered by the number of available females, and this is true in many other societies. Historically, the proliferation of wars to settle disputes left many more women alive, and the only way to provide them with male partners was to develop polygamous marriages. Some societies felt that without polygamy too many women would be left alone, thus contributing to less desirable situations, such as spinsterhood and prostitution. Since infant mortality rates were extremely high in some countries, it was also necessary to produce as many children as possible in the hope that more would survive. Polygamy became reality, too, because of the myths that surround menstruation and pregnancy. In some societies—and this is true even today—men would not cohabit with women who were menstruating or pregnant. Polygamy gave men choices of other mates when one was indisposed by nature.

THE MORMON EXPERIENCE WITH POLYGAMY

The Church of Jesus Christ of Latter-Day Saints established the doctrine of plural marriage in 1831. Polygamy was practiced in secret, however, for many years as protection against an American society that viewed the practice as heathen at best. Famed Mormon leader Brigham Young had twenty-seven wives and devoutly urged his followers to perpetuate the practice, even in the face of open public hostility. The experience of Mormon-style polygamy is chronicled in a book entitled *In My Father's House* by Dorothy Alfred Soloman, who grew up in a polygamous household consisting of seven wives and forty-eight children.

Soloman paints a picture of a household designed to please her father in every way, but also one in which the women were often in conflict about who had supremacy in his eyes. A definite pecking order existed among the wives, and some were not happy with their designated positions in that order. Some of the wives were only teen-agers when they married, but when older women in the household tried to become authority figures, they were not always welcomed by the younger women.

Writing poignantly about polygamy seen through a child's eyes, she writes, "I was already feeling sick to my stomach when my mother told me I couldn't sleep in her bedroom as I usually did to save bed space, because my father would spend the night with her. I moaned. It was just one 'cheat too many.' "

The Mormon experience with polygamy ended when it was outlawed in 1890, but some claim that the practice continues, however, very much underground. Soloman's father was ultimately gunned down by other Mormons from a rival polygamous sect, and she opted for a monogamous life-style after years of confusion over the issue. Apparently, through a young girl's eyes, polygamy forced Soloman constantly to feel displaced by the other wives and their offspring. She often felt empathy for her mother, although her mother appeared to be coping quite well.

There is a difference between how a child experiences polygamy and how a grown woman does. I interviewed women who live in polygamous households and found they exhibited a real sense of assurance and control. They mentioned how comforting it is to have cowives to rely on, instead of just a husband. In general, among these polygamous women I found a great sense of personal independence and little depression. However, I don't expect Americans will suddenly take up open polygamous life-styles, nor would I suggest that they do. This society does not have the social framework in which polygamy could flourish. To take this turn would only create more upheaval in family life. I mention polygamy in other cultures only to review how some systems make polygamy work and to show the difference in impact when multiple relationships are open.

POLYGAMY AMERICAN-STYLE

Estimates of the number of polygamous families in this country are hard to determine, for obvious reasons. One researcher, however, told me that she estimates almost five percent of the population is presently engaged in the practice. When you consider the numbers of people living in communes, or those who practice Eastern religions that sanction polygamy, not to mention the men and women who have quasi-polygamous life-styles, polygamy may be one of America's best-kept secrets.

Professor Joseph Scott, a sociologist, believes that polygamous relationships are very much a reality of modern-day American life and suggests that these relationships are submerged because of the fears of legal reprisals, the prevailing social mores, and the various government regulations that might keep certain of these families from receiving benefits.

I spoke with two American women who have quietly taken up the practice of polygamy. They believe there is a strong religious basis for the practice, but they also express a general dissatisfaction with the uncertainty of traditional American marriages. One head wife, whom I'll call Delores, entered a religious community in Washington, D.C., where polygamy was practiced, after a failed marriage. She made the choice because she thinks polygamous relationships make for a more stable family life.

Delores feels "safe" in her polygamous household because she knows at all times where her husband is. "He is either at work or with one of the other two wives whom I know very well. As head wife, I helped him select these other women, and we get along very well most of the time. I never feel the rejection I did in my first marriage, because we have a system where each wife has a specified time with our husband. We all are involved in scheduling the calendar with our husband, so no one feels threatened by any rivalry."

Her husband is supportive emotionally, and she feels a sense of security she has not had in other relations with men. "I focus more now on my own needs because I'm not worrying all of the time that he's going to leave and break up my family," Delores told me.

Another woman, Karen, a thirty-four-year-old physician, lives in a polygamous household with one other wife who she did not select. Her cowife is ten years younger than she, but they have been able to develop a rapport and spirit of togetherness. She chose a polygamous marriage because she was tired of struggling with "all the feelings of ownership and possession. I don't see my husband as a possession. We are a family unit and we make decisions that are best for everyone, and I like this."

Sex is considered private, says Karen, and she and her cowife don't discuss or compare notes about their sex lives with their husband. Each has her own bedroom, and he never enters either of their rooms. When they are to be with him, they go to his room. Neither wife interferes with this practice. Actually, not much sex occurs, she says, because the relationship is not based upon their physical union, but upon a spiritual basis instead.

It would be folly to paint polygamous households as idyllic, because they are not. However, from these two women's points of view, their lives are better now than when they were monogamous. Each spoke about the comfort of knowing what is happening around her, and the security that comes with knowing you have a place and a specific role. They both expressed firmly that polygamy works best when the women involved choose this life-style, rather than having it imposed upon them by a man. With choice, they say, comes power and some control over their lives. They also feel a strong sense of sisterhood with the other cowives. There is no rivalry, just support and understanding among them. The other woman is not an enemy, she is a friend.

Granted, most American women are not ready to adopt a polygamous life-style, even though their husbands may have secret families or long-term relationships with other women. However, these two women do not feel victimized or vulnerable, since their needs are considered and met in an orderly and predictable fashion. Polygamy helps them avoid the hurt and sense of betrayal that comes when multiple relationships are kept secret.

In this country, women grow up with the notion that men are basically polygamous but will change once married or commmitted to one woman, despite continual evidence to the contrary. In addition, American society facilitates mobility, making multiple relationships even easier for those men and women who thrive on them: It is no great feat for a man or woman whose job requires extensive travel to have two or more relationships at the same time. Who is the wiser? It is this style of "sharing" that I call polygamy American-style. While Americans generally frown on societies where a man is allowed more than one wife, we just exchange knowing smiles when we hear about a neighbor's husband who for all intents and purposes has another family on the other side of town. Is there any real difference between this guy who slips and slides between his two "families" and the Indian man who regularly visits his concubine and children?

Listen to this story, told to me by an attractive forty-four-year-old woman: " 'I'm having difficulty financially,' a young woman said to me on the phone. 'I don't want to start any trouble, but your husband simply won't return any of my phone calls. You see we have this four-month-old daughter, and I've got to get some kind of support just to get by.' "

As this woman, who I'll call Margaret, related her story to me, it was clear that it was still a difficult situation for her to grasp. Here was her husband, a successful executive at a prominent firm in town, who apparently had told all kinds of half-truths to this young woman in order to gain her trust. Now, she was in need with a young child, and he no longer wanted to be bothered. The thrill was gone. When Margaret confronted him, he said he felt ashamed at the mess he had created.

"I didn't feel that you cared or loved me anymore," he told his wife. "I'm getting older, and it means more to me now to know that I have what it takes. I didn't intend for this thing with this girl to go on very long, but then she got pregnant and I felt scared and ashamed."

Margaret admitted that, even after her discovery, she still loved her husband and wanted very much to save their marriage. He said he wanted the same thing and was willing to enter therapy with her. Today they are separated, Margaret says, but they still see each other. Obviously, their relationship has changed a great deal, but with four teen-agers, she is determined to find a way to keep some semblance of a family life.

This is a classic example of the man in his forties feeling very insecure about his desirability and entering into an affair with a younger woman to bolster his sagging ego. In his case, he wanted to end his affair and save his marriage, but many men do not end their affairs. Then, wives must either learn to live with it or sever the marital ties.

The triangle is not new to romance; it's just that today men don't always feel compelled to give up one of their loves when their duplicity comes out into the open. The only thing "new" about affairs is that now people don't try nearly as hard as in the past to keep them strictly undercover activities.

Many married men have always reserved for themselves "a night out with the boys," which usually meant an evening bowling with buddies from work or a game of all-night poker at a friend's house. Few worldly wives can take comfort in these excuses today. They probably hear single girl friends complain that all they meet at the clubs are married men who are perfectly willing to admit it. What woman on the single scene hasn't heard a married man's enticement to try him out because "my wife and I have an understanding?" Translated, this means that he does whatever he wants whenever he wants and still enjoys the benefits of a family life when he so chooses.

Who goes with whom is the stuff of office gossip and always has been. Only the truly innocent believe that office romance is a game for singles only. In addition, business travel has probably, unwittingly, encouraged both men and women to become involved in long-standing relationships in various cities. I know of married men and women who have what I call "office wives and husbands." These are generally close associates or even people on their own staffs who have every legitimate reason to join them for long lunches or accompany them on business trips. This is not to suggest that men and women who work together always necessarily play together, but the wise spouse should remember that familiarity doesn't *always* breed contempt. For some, this arrangement is very convenient and cozy. It's a good choice for men and women who are married and want to stay that way, because such a relationship has recognizable boundaries—from nine to five and when they are out of town the relationship is on; at all other times the marriage of record is sacrosanct. A married friend told me that the office romance is a perfect outlet for her need for "fun and games"; it doesn't require the changes in patterns that most affairs entail. She and her lover can meet at a friend's apartment or at an out-of-the-way hotel during the day when she would normally be at work. They also can plan special all-nighters for out-of-town meetings.

"Your husband never suspected?" I asked her once.

"No, he didn't," she said. "He was real hung up on having me home by a certain time in the evening, so this way everything I did was during work time and nothing changed at home. My lover was also married and enjoyed playing the role of the dutiful husband—you know, always home on time and strictly family activities for the weekend. Our affair allowed him to keep up this act and still have me on the side for excitement."

Gossip and jealousy in the office were more difficult to handle than either of the spouses, my friend pointed out.

"My lover had a pretty high position, so someone was always upset with him about something or other. At these times, my buddies would tell me about the stories going around about the two of us. Fortunately, we had been friends since college and occasionally socialized as couples, so our closeness could easily have been explained if the talk had somehow reached either of our mates. This affair might have gone on forever," my friend said wistfully. "Because we were really getting very close. I did feel like his other wife, and I came to resent that feeling. His wife was getting the benefits of a more contented spouse, and I got only a few stolen hours here and there. He admitted that I helped keep his marriage going, but he made me less content with mine. After a while resentments start building up and festering just like they do in a marriage, and who needs two marriages?"

Several people I talked to about affairs and their ultimate affect on marriage described the affair as a means of propping up the marriage—in other words, making this so-called monogamous relationship bearable. A forty-two-year-old man, married for twenty-three years and a grandfather of three, said that he had had other women throughout most of his marriage. Dan said that he had grown up in an all-female household "surrounded by bras and panties all my life," and, once an adult, he had felt the need to control the women in his life in order to keep them from controlling him.

"One day you realize your partner has ceased to grow as you have," Dan said. "Something is missing, so you go out and shop around to find what you need. I lie often to hide the truth from my wife, because I don't want to hurt her. Sometimes I would like to tell her, but she is so traditional, so closed-minded. The other woman actually helps my marriage: I begin to appreciate my wife when I have others to support my needs. I get feedback and support from my other woman; she listens and soothes my wounds."

Asked if he thought monogamy was possible for him under any circumstances, he replied, "I've never been monogamous. For a short period of time when my wife was pregnant I didn't stray, but that's the only time. No one woman has ever had me one hundred percent."

The reasons men have affairs are legion, and any analyst worth his or her salt will give you some psychological explanation for the fact that so many men feel it their inherent sexual right to have more than one woman. What surprises me is that in this day and time women still feel that they can concoct some magic potion that will make the men in their lives immune to sharing. This kind of woman wants to sprinkle the potion on her man so he'll suddenly lose interest if he is already involved with another woman. Whatever statistics one might choose to believe, in general, the percentage of men who admit that they cheat on their wives is about fifty percent. A survey cited in *Beyond the Male Myth,* by Anthony Pietropinto and Jacqueline Simenauer, went even further and concluded that "two thirds said they would cheat under certain circumstances."

Men have no monopoly on extramarital relations. Statistics also show that the number of married women seeking sexual partners outside of marriage is on the increase. While married women usually cite the need for emotional fulfillment as a reason for their affairs, men often say that their sexual needs are neglected at home. However, the female's tendency to get fixated on the emotional side of an affair can jeopardize her marriage, whereas few men will admit that they lose emotional control in their outside situations. When men allow themselves to fall in love with the other woman, they are prone to leave the marriage. For example, in the marriage of Vinny and Maria both partners were cheating, but it was Maria who kept things under control while Vinny fell in love and wanted to leave.

"We got married very young," Maria said. "We had known each other all through school, so I hadn't really had a chance to experience a lot of other men. After about three years of marriage, I felt like I was missing something—I started casually seeing other guys, but nothing too serious. But then I started seeing this man about fourteen years older than I, and it was clear from the start that he was going to be more than a lover, not that the sex wasn't good, because it was. He just gave me something my husband wasn't; he became my best friend."

As Maria described her marriage, the disappointment in her voice and expression was poignant. She had believed in the happily-ever-afters. She was now faced with the reality of sharing a life with a man with whom she has very little in common except a shared background (both Italian and Catholic), and two children. She decided that the only way to continue this marriage was to find some solace for herself with someone else. Having affairs allows her to tolerate what has become an empty marriage, but one she wants to hold on to all the same.

"My boyfriend was married, too, with four children and a wife who was virtually an alcoholic," Maria went on. "This was his first affair, and we fantasized often about being together on a permanent basis, but I can't honestly say that I ever seriously considered breaking up my home. He eventually divorced, but we started to drift apart. During this same period, I discovered that my husband was having an affair, too, with someone I knew. It got out of hand for him, though, and he came home one day and told me he was leaving.

"I wasn't working and didn't know which way to turn when he packed up," she said. "It felt like I had been kicked in the stomach. I was hurt, because regardless of what I had done with other men, I had never threatened to leave the marriage. I was determined to get him back: I confronted her once when I found them together, and what does he do? When I tried to go after her, he tried to protect her instead of consoling me."

After several more confrontations and physical violence, Maria did get Vinny to come home, but before long he was back with his girl friend. Maria decided to seek counseling, even though her husband refused to go. He tried again to break away from his girl friend and come home, but soon after his second return, she overdosed on sleeping pills in an attempt to win him back. Her suicide attempt, however, did not keep Vinny from once again making a commitment to his marriage. Maria said that things were never the same after their three years of seesawing back and forth.

"I always felt betrayed," she admitted. "He was ready to walk out on me, and I never would have done that to him. We're still together, but it's not good. I don't know if there is such a thing as a great marriage. I'm still not happy; I've learned to live with it. I see another man now and then, but not that often. When I go out now, I don't even bother to take my rings off. What difference does it make?"

Maria's plaintive "What difference does it make?" suggests to me a woman who has given up, not only on men, but on herself. There had been too much pain in all the wrangling back and forth with her husband. Contentment in the arms of the other men in her life had eluded her, and she had given up the notion that "maybe this time will be the last time, maybe this man will make me happy." There is no denying that the discovery that a spouse is having an affair is a wrenching experience, but women cannot allow this kind of pain to immobilize them or make them give up on themselves.

When the man in your life says, "Hey, look, you are a swell lady, but I have found someone else," the temptation is to believe that the woman must be a goddess. Just as Maria was, you may become consumed with the other woman, blocking out that the real problem is with your man. It's so easy to concentrate on how another woman has taken something from you, because it buys you some time before you have to face the fact that no man has an affair because some woman tricked him into it. Some men would have us believe that they fell into the hands of some Circe-like creature who dragged him away and kept him enthralled in her embrace. Women often accept such half-baked explanations because it's easier than confronting the truth.

When my husband told me that he had fallen in love with someone else, the ensuing days were truly bleak. I had built my world around him, and he was daring to tear it apart. It has taken me years to realize that no one should have that kind of control over another's life. In my work, I tell women there are no secret programs or formulas to ensure a pain-free life. No pill can make the headaches of romance go away. What women can do, though, is to learn to make decisions more carefully about the kinds of situations they will participate in. When a woman becomes more comfortable taking control of her life, the foibles of romance become less overwhelming. Having a man or not having one is no momentous concern for women who are confident of their own self-worth.

CHAPTER 4

Basic Approaches to Man Sharing

If it were sufficient to love, things would be too easy.
The more one loves, the stronger the absurd grows. It
is not through lack of love that Don Juan goes from
woman to woman. It is ridiculous to represent him as
a mystic in quest of total love.

Whence each woman hopes to give him what no other
has ever given him. Each time they are utterly wrong
and merely manage to make him feel the need of that
repetition.

"At last," he said, "but once more I have given you
my love, why should it be essential to love rarely in
order to love much?"

—ALBERT CAMUS
on Don Juanism

SHARING—THE ONLY
CHOICE FOR SOME

Most people willingly accept the idea that social mores have
changed since the late 1960's, but many still are reluctant to
examine what those changes mean for women and their social life-styles. The fact is that people are staying single longer,
and more and more singles have become part of the na-
tion's social fabric. The confirmed bachelor is no longer the
neighborhood oddity, and so-called old maids are not necessarily old anymore. What then does all of this mean for
the monogamous female who feels out of step with society

because she can't find an exclusive relationship? Some women have become frustrated with their plight and have quietly made the decision that sharing a man with other women may be the only way to sexual fulfillment.

This news should not be shocking to anyone in 1986, but each time I mention man sharing as an alternative life-style, I get quizzical stares or looks of disgust. Even after twenty years of social change, Americans still have rigid views about female sexuality. Sexual pleasure for women is still most often discussed in relation or response to male sexuality. It's still difficult, especially for men, to fathom that a woman might enjoy sex for sex's sake, just as he always has.

Sex is used in our society as a means of control. Men have understood this for centuries, but women have been socialized to believe they have no right to participate in this game except in disguised forms. For this reason, women are encouraged to be subtly seductive or passively controlling. However, with the sexual revolution, a few women have taken an entirely new view of their sexual rights.

To complicate matters, modern woman often finds herself in a double bind, because so few men are available to her emotionally and physically. That women outnumber men is one problem; another is the fact that many single men are uncomfortable with emotional connections. I know women who have relations with any number of men, but can't count on any one of them for much more than dinner and drinks and an occasional roll in the sack. Consequently, some women have decided to strike out on their own and explore sexual fulfillment in a variety of nontraditional ways. These women exude an attitude that translates into, "If that's the way they want it, I can play the same game."

Man sharing presents no real dilemma for some women because they have learned, after years of trying it the traditional way, that women can share as easily as men always have. A 1982 survey by *Playboy* magazine found that 70 percent of married women admit to having affairs; in the book *The Extramarital Connection,* by Lynn Atwater, 50 percent of married women admitted to having affairs. The reality is that Americans do honor monogamy mostly in the breach.

Women who choose sharing for themselves are unable to accept society's unwritten code, "Do as I say, not as I do." These women are controlled by no one's dictates other than their own. In fact, they would probably run from an exclusive relationship if one presented itself to them.

What kind of woman can pull off a shared relationship without the emotional upheavals we have come to expect from these situations? Those women I interviewed had some very basic characteristics in common. In each case they were self-confident women who had devoted much of their adult lives to the fulfillment of their social and sexual needs. Without a doubt, they had many years of social experience to back up their decision to share men when necessary. Each of these women had given monogamy a try—either through a marriage or live-in arrangement. But monogamy soon became cumbersome: They saw themselves either living by the man's rules or living by their own and experiencing, consequently, too much conflict in their relationships. Seeing themselves as some man's woman was clearly an uncomfortable position for these women, who insisted upon a separate identity to a point that most men, and even some women, would find extreme.

What struck me as most interesting about these women was their unabashed enjoyment of the company of men, even though they would never allow any one man to dominate their lives. They were always open to new encounters, whether one-night stands or the beginning of full-blown friendships. Some had special men in their lives with whom they enjoyed a constant relationship but, again, their relationships were never exclusive.

In general, these were women who had come to deeply mistrust exclusivity, even though they had not always felt this way. Some had developed a fear of commitment, which often seemed a mask of self-defense against the hurt they had experienced when they were monogamous. After repeated bumps with reality, many had accepted the nonexclusivity of men as a given, and conducted themselves accordingly. When men used noncommittal evasive language with them, they weren't bothered; they expected nothing else. Some might view this approach cynically, but these women swore that it worked for them.

Choosing several men with whom to share one's company is not for women who want the sanction of family, religion, or societal mores. Women who choose this course must understand clearly from the outset that they will never get approval for what they are doing. Those who feel the need to confess and tell all should forget about sharing as an option. This will only reinforce guilt feelings and cause deeper inner turmoil.

Perhaps the most significant characteristic of women who share by choice is their willingness to ignore society's myths about female sexuality as they seek fulfillment in many unconventional liaisons with the opposite sex. In the book *Women and Self-Esteem: Understanding and Improving the Way We Think and Feel About Ourselves,* authors Linda Sanford and Mary E. Donovan discuss the need for women to attack prevailing myths in order to find satisfying sexual relationships. To take this risky step, the authors say, "means unlearning rigid ideologies and lies, discovering what gives her pleasure, and taking the risk of pursuing self-discovery. It is no easy task, but for a fuller sense of self, she may decide it's worth the effort." Sharing a man willingly is not for the fainthearted. The constant struggle of juggling time and men and managing to overcome deeply ingrained feelings of competition and ownership can be unsettling even for women who are experienced in man sharing. But, for the women who embark on this course, there are many benefits.

Take, for example, Mandy, a thirty-eight-year-old married woman who believes that no woman should ever allow herself to be dependent on one man, even if he's a "fairly good husband." She described her marriage as basically solid after fifteen years, but one that hit a plateau some years ago, and nothing much had changed since then. Frustrated with her longing for romance and excitement, she chose to use the time she spent away from home on business travel as a means to set up other relationships that could provide for her what her husband would not. She had told him once what she needed from him: more flattery, time, and attention. He had laughed at her.

"Monogamy is an illusion in American society," she said emphatically. "For some reason women feel the need to keep this illusion going, but I don't. Most of the men I know have affairs with more than one woman, and I can't see why I shouldn't do the same thing. After all, it's only a sin if you think it is. I am not irresponsible with my family, and I do everything I can to keep my family happy and secure. My affairs aren't allowed to get out of hand, because I would never consider leaving my husband. I just feel the need to put my life together in a way that makes me happy, and that's what I do."

Mandy, who abhors the Victorian view of women as chaste and virtually asexual beings, said that "women need to stop expecting permission from men to be happy. It's their responsibility to make themselves happy in whatever fashion they can handle."

Mandy's first affair, which has lasted seven years, is now a solid friendship. She receives support spiritually, emotionally, and socially. Her friend adds to her life what her husband is just not willing to do right now. She calls her affairs "renewal experiences" that keep her spirits uplifted, thus allowing her to be a happier and more responsive wife and mother.

I am beginning to meet more and more single women who, like Mandy, refuse to limit themselves to one man, simply because they don't trust the outcomes of most so-called one-on-one relationships. They opt to keep the controls in their own hands while enjoying a full social life at the same time. Although they understand traditional mores, one man to one woman, they no longer believe that they are solely responsible for upholding such outdated rules.

Donna is a forty-four-year-old divorcée. After several years of practicing law, she decided to enroll part-time in a seminary. Committed to teaching religion at some point in her life, Donna feels no conflict with her deeply held spiritual values and the fact that she enjoys multiple sexual relationships. "I take an eclectic approach to Christianity and have real problems with the dogma in some Christian sects. People need to understand that the Christian ethic as written in the Bible reflects the cultural ethics that prevailed at the time of those doing the writing. We are hung up on monogamy only because we are socialized that way. If I had been brought up in a polygamous society, I might now be happy as one of several wives. Quite frankly, I don't think God cares how many husbands or wives you have, but I do think he cares how you treat them."

Twice married, Donna says that her perspective on men

and relationships has changed significantly as she has gotten older. "Young people have a tendency to be self-righteous. Women in this country have so many 'Thou shalt not's' piled upon them that often it's hard to crawl out. But now I'm arrogant enough to believe that I can do whatever I want on this planet without making justifications to anyone."

"Body buffing" is what Donna calls the encounters she designs with male friends when sex is all she has on her mind. "I have a couple of guys I can call to have my needs met. We are friends, but sex is included if we both desire it. One of these guys is attractive and quite a bit of fun, but he's definitely not husband material. If he calls and I'm available, we get together, but I certainly don't leave space for him, nor would I rearrange my life to make room for him."

She recently met a guy with whom she grew up and who she feels is husband material, and she's working "to get him together." Previously married, he is shy about any kind of commitment, but she says he really sets off her "man" alarm. "You know what I mean," she said, "when I see him, 'the fireworks go off.'" Her concern about this man is that he is "the 'classic closed' man. I have to jolt him every now and then by doing and saying things he considers outrageous."

Because she shares some common values with him—for example, both consider success important in life—Donna is willing to invest some time in him, but not to the exclusion of other men. In addition to the friends she relies upon for body buffing, from time to time she also sees a minister with whom she can share her spiritual beliefs. "He's very conservative, but I don't believe in telling any man all of my business. I don't ask any questions and don't expect any."

Her advice to women is to stop doing so much therapy with men. "I see women wringing themselves out over men who need doctors not lovers. I refuse to spend my life doing therapy on any man. Most of it isn't necessary anyway. I hear women whine about their men not opening up to them in the way they desire. We impose too much on men. I don't think we need them to understand everything we do, just as long as they stay out of our way."

I found Donna to be a well-adjusted woman with her own healthy convictions. She had tried it the way society dictated—monogamously—and now she was designing her own way and finding more satisfaction, less guilt and depression.

Jane, a pretty, single forty-three-year-old redhead from Kansas, also told me that juggling has become a most enjoyable way of life for her. "I have a young man about twenty-eight years old whom I adore but can't get to see that often because of his job. We see each other when we can and have a wonderful time. He remembers my birthday with lavish gifts and generally treats me like a very special lady. Someday I think we might be able to work out a permanent relationship, but that day is not now, for any number of reasons. I see other men from time to time. I have a sixty-five-year-old man who also treats me royally. He's a widower and enjoys having the company of a woman so much younger than he. We travel together, and he functions in many ways as a professional mentor. He's opened many doors for me in my career and makes few demands socially. We genuinely like each other, and spending time with him is something I look forward to."

Jane is a woman of vast contradictions. I interviewed her several times, and each encounter gave me a completely different view of her. On the one hand, she is a consummate professional—articulate, assertive, and very much a reflection of the Establishment. And at other times, she is an outspoken inconoclast giving deference to none of life's conventions. When she is in her professional role, her dress is as crisp as her speech. Her black suit, high-collared blouse, and pearls seem more to fit the image of the high-level executive she actually is than do her conversations, which are often peppered with ribald stories about her sexual pursuits. After one of our meetings, I remember laughing when I thought about this charming woman with an aristocratic air telling me stories about leaving her office early one day because one of her lovers had called and wanted to make love that afternoon. She seems to care little about the dissimilarities in her image and her life-style, and, I think, secretly enjoys how shocking she can be to others.

Jane is very straightforward about what she wants from any man in her life. Her immediate priorities are her career and getting a son from her first marriage through college. Marriage is not a must for her, even though she hasn't ruled it out. And since she is not hung up on finding a spouse or building a family, she is freer than some younger women simply to enjoy a man's company, even when commitments are impossible. She also believes strongly that a man can be a woman's best friend. Her ex-husband is both a sometime lover and professional confidant. She can commiserate with him on any subject and continues to view him as important in her life. They chose to end their marriage many years ago, but decided to salvage a friendship that had always been solid and rewarding for both of them.

There are those people who would quickly label Mandy, Donna, and Jane as promiscuous, but who is to judge? The definition of promiscuity implies lack of restrictions and discrimination. Yet, each woman has standards of behavior that she has set for herself. For example, Jane has definite rules about who among her male friends she allows to meet her children, and no men are allowed to spend the night in her home. From the contentment she exudes about herself, her way works for her.

Another woman, named Brenda, a thirty-eight-year-old divorcée from Minneapolis, related experiences that were very similar to Jane's. She had been on the carousel of romance many years, hoping each time for a commitment, only to be disappointed again and again. Brenda talked wistfully about a college romance that she had hoped would end in marriage. Bill, whom she says was probably her first and only true love, eventually married someone else. He now lives the two-kid suburban life-style that she so long had envisioned for herself. But Brenda no longer is waiting for love to happen to her.

"I realized that as long as I sat around my house hoping for a change," Brenda said, "that nothing was really going to happen for me. I had been struggling with a complicated, long-standing situation with one guy, but his constant confusion kept me drained. I woke up one day realizing that I wasn't having any fun anymore. You would be surprised how this realization changed things for me. I started noticing the men who had been trying to get my attention at work. It seemed suddenly that there were men all around me whom I just hadn't noticed, because I was always so worked up about this other guy. I got into a little business on the side selling health products and met two terrific men through my business consultations. I'm not in love with either of these men, but I do like each of them for different reasons. Why shouldn't I enjoy myself with each of them when I can?"

Women like Brenda rarely feel victimized, because they don't enter relationships with any preconceived expectations. One woman told me that when red flags go up after a few encounters with a particular man, she simply moves on. There is no cause for wringing of hands and tears, because she always feels that she has other options. Thus, she said, she is free to engage in "sometimey" affairs with men she would never consider marrying, even though they may be great fun for the moment. Women of choice do not bed hop indiscriminantly. They may be involved with several men, but there is often some longevity in their relationships.

I cannot emphasize enough the great sense of relief and ultimate freedom women can experience if they stop seeing each man they meet as a potential mate. Women lose out on some potentially interesting gentlemen and some very worthwhile encounters when they restrict themselves to husband hunting. I ask women to try a new approach slowly, just to see how it works for them: The next time you meet a guy, forget for a minute how tall he is, how much money he might make, or what color his eyes are. Then, engage him in a conversation to see where his head is and if anything about him is appealing. Only then should you decide whether you'd like to see him again or not. Men can be approached from many perspectives, and women who know this rarely complain about how few good men there are. Following are a few new ways to look at men that will make sharing more manageable emotionally and may widen the scope of possibilities for satisfaction in your life.

STOPGAPS AND FILL-INS

A man who is a sometime escort, occasional dinner companion, or even a summer lover is what I term a stopgap or fill-in. It's clear from the beginning that he will not be a long-term relationship, but he can get you through a lonely night. With this person, there are no discussions about building a life together, other women, or "Where do we go from here?" Both of you take the relationship for what it is—short-term commitment that will go on only as long as you both are having fun.

A woman once described to me a situation that clearly illustrated the concept of a stopgap or fill-in. She was in a clothing store one day, and a man obviously wishing to make conversation asked her if it was possible to buy auto paint in the store. They chuckled awhile about the fact that they were in a clothing store, and she found herself physically attracted to the man. A professor at a local university, she was disappointed when she learned that he was a mechanic. She immediately feared that the intellectual stimulation she so treasured in men would surely be lacking. However, she accepted a few dates with him anyway and discovered that he was a warm and sensitive lover whose company she enjoyed. She rationalized that she could get intellectual stimulation from some of her other friends, so there was no need to give up this man just because he had a few shortcomings. "It's not going to last forever," she told me, "but I sure am going to enjoy it for the time being."

The time being is what stopgaps and fill-ins are all about. It's sharing one or several interests with someone you can enjoy for a while. A future together is not the issue.

À LA CARTE

The à la carte method allows you some flexibility with your social relations with men. No longer tied to the notion that only one man can satisfy all of your needs, you can go about selecting different companions for different reasons. Your tennis partner might hate the country/western saloon you frequent on Friday nights, so you choose someone else to accompany you there. And Harry, who loves football games and autumn picnics, may loathe the political banquets your job requires that you attend. This is where Bob comes in, because he loves black-tie events and knows all the right politicos in town.

The à la carte method ensures a woman that she has a variety of companions to call on for different reasons. These may not necessarily be romantic liaisons; the man involved may be just a good friend or a sometime lover. The point is that you usually get together around a specific task or activity, and he doesn't feel used, because you provide similar support for him. This approach is especially useful to professional single women who must have an escort for various events, and being paired off is important in some professional environments. I know women who make this work by even borrowing a friend's husband or brother when an escort is critical. If the arrangement is understood by all parties involved, there is rarely any negative fallout.

I'm certainly not suggesting that women sleep with all of their friends or companions. À la carte adds flexibility and interest to a woman's life even when Mr. Wonderful is not on the scene.

THE BLAST FROM THE PAST

A few years ago, I embarked on an ill-fated relationship with a man who now is so much older and wiser that I sometimes wish we could try it again. We all have people in our lives who we wish we could put on hold and go back and pick them up when the time is right. Although we can't freeze people in time, we may get the chance to consider them a second time around, when for various reasons the atmosphere may be more favorable.

Blasts from the past usually turn up when they are experiencing a lonely period in their own lives. They reach back into their memories and remember some charming someone from some happier time and determine to see what this person is up to now. The approach can be awkward, especially when a great deal of time has elapsed since they last spoke. The call usually begins with something like, "I was thinking of you today, because I saw someone crossing the street who reminded me of you. I thought I would call to see how you are doing." Then the person waits for a response to see if the other is receptive to any further conversation. If the answer is a warm one, the suggestion to get together usually follows. If the response is lukewarm, pleasantries are exchanged and both wiggle out of the conversation without ever bringing up getting together. This cat-and-mouse game protects the person calling from rejection. It's safer than calling up and saying, "I miss you," and risking the other person's ire.

So, if that old boyfriend calls and says he's in town for a few days, don't get hung up on everything that went wrong the last go around. Give it another whirl; the extra effort might be worth it.

THE LONG-INTERVAL MAN

During those periods in your life when nothing really exciting seems to be in the offing, the Long Interval Man can come in handy. This man is a do-or-die buddy who remains in the recesses of your life for many years. He may have been a lover at one time, and after the glow of romance diminished, you both decided that you would rather have a little of each other than none at all. He's the man you can call on when you are in a jam, for you know he will help if he can, with no strings attached. You two may even get together sexually from time to time, but this clearly is not the focus of your relationship. Once you are married or in a committed relationship, he may remain in the background. Then lunches and drinks together and long chats on the phone may be the mainstay of the relationship. But whatever happens to either of you, it's safe to assume that you are there for each other, no matter what.

The significant feature of the Long Interval Man is that he is connected to you spiritually. The best description is probably to call it a brother-sister kind of love. You have probably seen each other through many crises, even with other people. In spite of all that has happened, though, the relationship is still strong and reliable.

THE FRIEND

When I talk to women about the importance of having male friends, they usually have trouble figuring out how you can relate to a man if not sexually. Female friends can be phone buddies and gossip pals, but they never consider men for just friendly purposes. What an injustice to men to think sex is all they are good for! Women often tell me that men have no interest in developing friendships with women, unless sex has a definite role in the relationship. I'm sure in many cases this is true, but if you persevere with a guy you know you like but have no interest in sexually, often a rewarding relationship can follow.

There are two problems with having male friends. The first is thinking from the start that you can negate the sexual energy that is natural between man and woman once you embark upon a platonic relationship. You can't wipe it away but, with effort, you can neutralize it and build a friendship. You might dicuss how sex would change your relationship in a way that neither of you really wants. After this, it can remain a private joke between the two of you. The other problem with adult friendships, according to sociologist Peter Stein of H. H. Lehman College, is that the whole notion of friendship among adults remains a rather fuzzy concept in our society. "Our culture expects people to pair off, but where does friendship fit? For instance, is it okay to compete with friends for the opposite sex or success? These are questions that inhibit the growth of friendships as we get older." In addition, competition short-circuits many friendships among women. "If three female friends meet one guy they all like, what are they to do?" he queries.

Stein says that the most important factor in building friendships with men is to give yourself time and to expect no instant relationships. "Openness, sharing, and acceptance are the most important ingredients, and after that you just need a little time."

THE IMPORTANCE OF NONROMANTIC FRIENDSHIPS

Harriette McAdoo, a professor of social work who has devoted much of her research to issues surrounding single women and their life-styles, observes that nonromantic friendships with men can provide the much-needed support that many single female parents need to get them through some difficult situations. In fact, many of the women I interviewed discuss "uncle"-type friends who help them when they need it. McAdoo's research shows that older men tended to be more receptive to these kinds of relationships.

When sex enters a relationship, the placid waters of friendship may begin to ripple. Sociologist Dr. Lawrence Gary explains that sex gets in the way of what could be very workable platonic relationships. "Women and men have to realize that relationships don't have to include sex to be satisfying. For instance, a man could be very helpful to many single mothers by helping with the kids or assisting her with household repairs, but if sex gets into it, problems usually result."

I was heartened recently to hear of a men's group in Los Angeles whose purpose is to adopt a family of a single mother and provide a male role model for the children. Dr. James

May, who heads the group, said that sex was the least of his concerns when he organized these men. "The idea is to relate to the family as a whole," he said. "People are people, and I'm sure that sexuality is sometimes a factor, but our main goal is to help out with the children and expose them to a different way of life." There are similar male groups in Washington, D.C., Philadelphia, and other urban centers.

Male friends have gotten me out of more tight situations than I care to mention, and I have on numerous occasions reciprocated. One friend, whom I can call anytime night or day, comes to mind. He has married during our relationship, but his wife is fully aware that I consider her husband one of my dearest friends and confidants. He advises me on a host of topics, including other men, and believe me, you can get no better advice on male behavior than from another male. When you are friends, you can trust that the advice is objective and unbiased, and when he turns to you with troubles with his own lady love, you get the chance to return the favor.

Man sharing is not always about sex, even though it's more titillating for people to believe this is so. For example, women who marry or cohabitate with divorced men who have children will often have to share this man with his previous family. But some women are so possessive that they can't even accept the time a man spends with his children. It's no wonder, then, that platonic friendships with men are so hard for women who are hung up on exclusivity. Women who overlook the value of platonic relationships with men are missing a most rewarding experience and forget that sometimes the best suitors and husbands are those men who were friends first.

Women must learn that the man of their dreams may not always be available. This, however, is no reason to sit and complain about all the wonderful things you could do if you only had a man in your life. Exploring some of the foregoing kinds of relationships will allow you to have male companionship, but not necessarily a commitment. Women who put their lives on hold while they wait for commitments are not in touch with reality—and clearly are missing out.

CHAPTER 5

What Happens When You Don't Accept Reality

O God, give us serenity to accept what cannot be changed, courage to change what should be changed, and wisdom to distinguish the one from the other.
—REINHOLD NIEBUHR

The question women ask me perhaps more than any other is how they can change a man who believes in sharing himself with several women. The answer is, they can't. Married women, in particular, say they refuse to share their husbands, but in the next breath they tell me of their husband's involvement with another woman. Although most women openly oppose the idea of sharing, many admit that they participate in these relationships nonetheless. This is because their willingness to be monogamous may have little effect on a man's behavior. His attitude may be, "If you want to be monogamous, so be it," but this doesn't mean he will do the same.

Women who persist in the notion that monogamy is the only way of life are the women who collapse in emotional upheaval when they find themselves in shared situations. These are the women who see sharing as something being done to them; clearly, it is not a choice. More often than not, these women are still clinging to the idea of one man to one woman. These are women I call women in dilemma.

Several years ago, the media highlighted for months the plight of one single woman who could not accept the fact that she was sharing her lover with another women. Jean Harris was disturbed enough by the situation to consider suicide and ended up killing her longtime lover, Dr. Herman Tarnower. Harris is but one example of the hundreds of women who each day decide they can take no more and take matters into their own hands. Recently, thirty-two-year-old Leanita McClain, the first black woman to serve on the *Chicago Tribune*'s editorial board, decided that life had lost all meaning for her after her plans to marry fell through. Previously divorced, and troubled for many years by chronic depression, McClain chose on the tenth anniversary of her broken marriage to end her life by taking an overdose of sleeping pills. After several glowing paragraphs about this remarkable woman's achievements, the newspaper article announcing her death simply said, "It is reported that she was depressed over a man." Although the stories of most women's pain and anguish over broken love affairs rarely hit the papers, my experience indicates that more and more women feel they can no longer cope with the deceptions of their romances.

Unlike the women in the previous chapter, who found monogamy wanting and had chosen sharing as a way of life, women in dilemma generally cannot function sexually unless they believe a relationship is monogamous. Or they may decide to relate sexually to only one man, and when he sees others, they become depressed, although they never really consider leaving the relationship.

Some married women hide from the fact that they are sharing their husbands. They deny the reality so they can continue in the relationship. On the other hand, some men will go to great lengths to conceal their philandering so their mates can continue to believe their relationship is monogamous. This is enough for some women, even if they suspect that the man sees others from time to time. However, these same women would never think of seeing another man because "it wouldn't be right." They generally are concerned only with how they can bring enough pressure to bear on their men to make them stop seeing other women. The sad truth is that there is virtually nothing a woman can do to alter a man's sexual behavior. What she can do, though, is change her own behavior. One of the first steps for a woman in a dilemma about sharing is to follow her instincts where men are concerned.

FOLLOWING YOUR INSTINCTS

A woman called me one day during my radio show to tell me of a recent encounter with a dashing stranger. She and the stranger met at a local disco, and it was love at first sight. They danced, she said, as if they had always danced together and talked like true soul mates right from the beginning. However, despite being totally caught up in the headiness of the evening, there was something about the man that nagged at her. She noted that he said some things that sounded like lines she had heard before and seemed in a hurry to get intimate, but the words sounded so good she chose to ignore how smooth and well-rehearsed he seemed. They wined and dined and slept together, and at last they exchanged phone numbers and said, "Au revoir." She called him two days later at his office, wondering why she hadn't heard from him. He was unavailable, so she left her number. But he didn't return her call. Finally, she decided to call his home number, and a woman answered the phone. When he came to the phone, he said the woman was a roommate but that he would call her the next day from the office. Needless to say, she never heard from him again. Even though she knew that the woman was not really just a roommate, she desperately wanted to believe it—to hold on to the illusion that he was available.

Another woman named Sarah told me how excited she was about Charles, a single man she had met through friends. After a few weeks of dating, he began telling her how he had fallen on some "hard times" and was about to lose his apartment. Things weren't going well on the job either, and he thought he might be laid off soon. She felt sorry for him immediately and offered to let him move in with her. After he moved in, she discovered that it was nice having a man around the house, even though Charles kept erratic hours while "he was trying to put his life back together."

They rarely did anything together, because he couldn't afford it, but he spent many hours outside of the apartment "just hanging around with the guys." This situation continued for a while, until Sarah noticed Charles was becoming less affectionate and less communicative. When asked, however, he always assured her of his love. She knew something was wrong, but didn't want to face it. The idea of losing him and having him move out was much too painful. One day, she forgot some important papers for the office and rushed home to get them, after repeated calls home and no answer from Charles. When she arrived, Charles was there with another lady, and Sarah was forced into a reality she had tried hard to avoid.

Sometimes your instincts will so unsettle you that you will go searching for concrete evidence of your suspicions. Take the forty-eight-year-old woman I spoke to in a beauty salon, who said she had found a hotel receipt in her husband's wallet. When she confronted him, he said that he had allowed a single friend to use his credit card to surprise a new lady love. I could tell, as she related her story, that she didn't believe it; she needed my confirmation of her worst suspicions. As we talked, she mentioned other changes in his behavior—a sudden surge in office overtime, for instance—and I realized that she had all the evidence she needed. She was hesitant, however, to make a decision about what to do.

We all have gut feelings that seem to crop up from nowhere but are often based in some reality that our conscious minds refuse to face. Be ever mindful of your gut reactions, because they are often a clue to what is bothering you about a situation. If you think for some reason that you are sharing the man in your life, you probably are.

In my professional experience, women always know when they are sharing. They choose to ignore the signs to forestall the pain and decisions they must make. This sets up feelings of helplessness, because they are unprepared to take necessary actions.

Women, then, need to develop constructive ways of dealing with sharing that don't leave us reacting hysterically. One way to begin is to express your feelings, then make specific plans for handling the situation, plans that will work for you, not against you.

If you are uncomfortable in shared relationships, you should not participate. Don't ignore obvious signs that you are sharing a man just to avoid the pain. Do not allow a clouded reality to leave you so vulnerable that you are unprepared to make decisions about your relationship that are in your best interest. If, though, you need definitive signs of sharing, following is a list of fairly reliable indicators that you are not the only woman in a man's life:

- He begins to go out more often by himself.
- He calls less frequently.
- After a whirlwind courtship, he cuts back on weekend commitments and opts instead for a night during the week.
- He decides it would be better to meet at your place than his.
- His night out with "the boys" stretches from late night to all night.
- He fusses more with his physical appearance, maybe even changing his style of dress or brand of cologne.
- He jumps when the telephone rings and rushes to answer it himself.
- You notice a marked increase in hang-up calls and wrong numbers.
- His travel schedule inexplicably changes, and he is missing often from his office for long stretches of time.
- Overtime at the office suddenly increases, but when you call, he's not there or claims he was somewhere doing research.
- The frequency of sex diminishes, or he has a sudden interest in experimentation.
- He starts coming home late and heads first to the bathroom to wash up instead of talking to you.
- He moves farther and farther away from you in bed.
- You notice more entertainment charges on credit cards, and he begins to have more trouble balancing the checkbook.

If more than half of these observations apply, prepare yourself for precarious footing in your relationship. In fact, you might well begin to determine some survival strategies of your own.

SURVIVAL STRATEGIES WHEN YOU ARE SHARING UNWILLINGLY

No event can cause the ground under a woman to shake faster than her discovery that a husband or lover is having an affair with another woman. The anger, hurt, and depression that overcome a woman during this time may cause her to denigrate herself and make her doubt her prospects for surviving the betrayal. Unfortunately, she may also begin questioning whether she, too, should take on other lovers. Considering sharing when the option has been foisted upon you is the least propitious time to think about its benefits. "I'll fix him by going out with someone else" is the familiar threat I hear from women as they reel from the blows of his faithlessness.

What you need to do first upon the discovery that your loved one is sharing is to decide unequivocally what it is you want from the relationship and how best you can get it. You notice I did not mention finding out what he wants, because as hard as this may be for you to believe, what his plans are or aren't needn't be that critical initially. Struggling to find out what he wants to do will only perpetuate your state of confusion and anxiety, and will give him all of the power, which is probably what got you into trouble in the first place. You can't begin to negotiate a truce with him until you do the following:

- Uncover your own personal sources of power in your relationship—and withdraw or withhold your assets, both tangible and intangible, until you get him into a compromising position.
- Allow yourself to express anger.
- Conserve your energy for constructive endeavors—for-

get following him and his other lady around or camping at her doorstep.
• Become comfortable with the idea of taking some risks.
• Learn to trust your intuition.
• Separate dreams and wishes from reality.
• Know when to compromise and when to stand firm.
• Have a good sense of timing.

Negotiation may seem a very clinical and unromantic tactic when used in terms of an intimate relationship, but we all must understand that with every relationship there is an unwritten contract. Tacit understandings are the hallmark of all human relationships, so you must make clear to your partner what your terms are. Being coy or hysterical when a man says he's leaving is foolish if you want the relationship to work. You must allow yourself the time to consider what you have at stake, understanding that ultimately you may have to get out. Letting go is perhaps the hardest part of the process, but it's an outcome you must come to grips with. I am reminded here of wise words: "If you want something badly enough, let it go. If it comes back to you, it's yours. If it doesn't come back, it was never yours in the first place." When you do your worst-case scenario, don't leave out the possibility that you may have to let him go.

According to psychologist Dr. Leota Tucker, married women who decide to continue their relationships after the discovery of an affair face a special set of problems. They must learn to cope with mixed feelings toward their husbands—feelings that may make it difficult, if not impossible, to relate to them sexually and emotionally. Coping with these negative feelings can be an ordeal since almost any stimulus can conjure up images of a husband with another woman. Dr. Tucker says coping with these unpredictable flashes or fantasies can be a herculean task. In fact, many women who had previously decided to stay with their husbands, often may leave when these images prove to be unbearable.

Women who are able to cope effectively with this emotional period of estrangement from their husbands report that they use it to think about what form they want their relationship to take in the future. They also use it to negotiate a new way of relating to their husbands. In many cases, women will attempt to rectify some of the inequities that have existed over the years. They may also attempt to restructure the relationship in a way that makes them feel less vulnerable and more secure. For *some* women, this will involve new financial arrangements that protect her in the event the marriage is dissolved. For others, the negotiation may take place around increased sharing of household chores or child-rearing responsibilities. Women in this situation must make time to work out their anxieties. If they don't find ways to release their frustrations, they may tend to take it out on themselves or others.

Singles often have a difficult time putting together a survival strategy when they discover they are sharing, because they may not understand exactly where they are in the relationship. For instance, a single woman who has seen a man only a few months has little at risk if he announces that he wants to see others. On the other hand, if a woman has been living with a man for many years, her reactions may be similar to a married woman's. It is interesting to note, however, that often women have similar reactions regardless of how much they have really invested in the relationship. I believe single women should always assume that a man is seeing others, until the two reach a point where exclusivity is expressly desired by *both*. Too many women impose monogamy upon themselves as soon as they meet a man they like, and this action sets them up for disappointment if he sees their relationship from a different vantage point. Realize that if you choose monogamy without ever discussing it with your partner, there is little you can say if he tells you that exclusivity was never part of the deal.

Self-imposed monogamy is a trap women set up for themselves, according to former psychotherapist Jo Katherine Page, who specialized in therapy for women. "Sharing doesn't come as easily to women as it does to men," she said. "Too often women choose sharing in reaction to what a man does, and this approach never works. Women need to understand that they should have other men in their life all along, not just in reaction to a crisis. I'm not talking just about lovers, but friends. You have male friends before this lover or husband, why drop them?"

Women should have an array of different people in their lives, and I will never understand women who seek to isolate themselves from other men and even from their female friends as soon as a special man enters the picture. He should be only part of your life, not its primary focus.

HOW LONG TO GO WITH HALF A LOAF

"When in doubt do nothing": This is my advice for any woman who is sharing and contemplating breaking up with her man. Stay with it, and wrestle with the pros and cons until it's pretty evident to you that you don't want to go on any longer in this fashion. This involves plotting and planning how your needs can be met if you stay or what your needs will be if you go off on your own. Your best interests should always be your guide.

If you are married or have been in a live-in relationship for some time, there are three options you have: 1) stay, having renegotiated the terms of the relationship; 2) stay, emotionally divorcing yourself from him and perhaps taking a lover on the side; or 3) leave. Many factors may be considered as you try to decide whether it's worth it to stick it out, and love may be the least of those considerations. At this time, it's easy to get stymied around the wrong issues. While you may be curious about your man's other woman, forget about trying to find the answers to these kinds of questions: Is he in love with the other woman? Does he still love me? Is he in love with both of us? What does he want?

In addition, try not to spend a great deal of time fantasizing about the other woman. Is she more attractive and/or more intelligent? Does she have the "power" to convince him to leave home? What does she have that I don't? Invest your energies into those practical determinations that will ensure your own mental and physical well-being. Worrying about the other woman will sidetrack you and make worse an already bad situation.

Sometimes women tell me that they have too much financially invested with a man to leave him, so they opt for a quasi-separation within their home. Yet for the public, they are still together. Children also may be the reason they decide to stay, though little ones can be very perceptive and will sense that something is amiss. None of these reasons is a good one for staying, however, when your own mental health is threatened.

A friend of mine decided to remain in a marriage clearly going down the drain because she had become so accustomed to an affluent life-style and she felt she couldn't maintain it on her own. Soon, she developed eczema, a skin disorder her doctor ascribed to nerves. She became compulsively driven and constantly anxious—behavior not part of her usual demeanor.

After enduring for a while, she concluded that her health was more important than a fancy car and a sable mink coat and she sought marital counseling. Through counseling, she was able to sort out more effectively what values were important to her and ultimately made the decision to terminate her marriage.

For singles, even though the consequence of breaking up may not be as dire as for those who are married or cohabitating, the emotional effects may be the same, especially if a great deal of time and energy have gone into the relationship. The problem, though, for some singles is that they are often unable to differentiate between serious relationships and those that are more casual.

The first task for a single person is to decide how serious this relationship is. If the man has told you up front that he just wants to free-lance and he only calls you on a Tuesday or Wednesday night, if he shows little interest in you beyond the sexual, if you don't feel you can count on him in an emergency or when you need him just to talk, it's clear that you don't have much upon which to build genuine intimacy. Understand the difference between casual dating and a relationship. You may decide that you can handle sharing on one level, but not another. Just be sure to base your decisions on reality. Use your common sense; no contract is binding without mutual agreement.

Take, for instance, a twenty-five-year-old woman who discovered for the third time in one year a man she had committed herself to was seeing other women. When pressed, she admitted that being exclusive was her choice, but she had no such agreement from him. With the realization that he was seeing others, she became depressed. After talking with her, it became apparent that she consistently misread what men told her and how they behaved toward her. Therefore, she continually wound up investing more in the relationship than they did. Her reactions were so extreme that she considered ending her life. All she had to do was terminate her misbegotten affairs and open her eyes to the real world.

When you can honestly say to yourself, married or single, that the give and take in a relationship with a man doesn't balance out and that you are always on the short end, you need to begin the process of phasing out.

HOW TO PHASE OUT

Washing that man right out of your hair can be a painful process, but not an impossible one. It's stressful no matter who does the leaving, but if you decide to pull out, the onus is on you to make the break stick. If you insist on clinging to worn-out memories of how things used to be, it will be harder. The struggle, though, is not over the good times, because if you are honest with yourself, the good times must have slacked off or you wouldn't be at this point. Fear of loneliness and change are at the root of your troubles, and this is to be expected.

Most of the women who attend man-sharing workshops do so because they are angry, depressed, and very much in conflict. Conflict arises when you know that leaving is the only answer, but you fear the consequences of choosing to take care of yourself. For women who have been in relationships a long time, the single life is both awesome and mind-boggling. Many openly wonder if they might be better off putting up with sharing their mates with others rather than subjecting their psyches to the humiliation of the singles marketplace. (And a marketplace is what it seems to women uninitiated in the rights of the modern dating game.)

What I offer to women in sharing situations who decide to get out is a method that enables them to leave with their egos and confidence intact. It's a process that should be taken a step at a time with the following thoughts in mind:

What Happens When You Don't Accept Reality

1. Begin by asking yourself, "What's the worst thing that will happen if I don't have this relationship? Will my life really stand still?"
2. You've heard this one before: You must let go of the old feelings before you can go on to new experiences. To let go you must mourn the loss. Give yourself space to cry and come to an understanding.
3. Find ways to stop thinking about him. You will have to actively work on this. Think about something else that has brought you pleasure. Whenever a thought of him occurs, think STOP as adamantly as you can. Also keep some type of tab on how often you think of him, so you'll notice the progress you're making.
4. Everytime you decide to go to the telephone to call him, think STOP. Then call someone else, like a friend. Or dial the number but hang up before there's a response.
5. When you find yourself thinking of the pleasant times together, STOP—and think of the times that made you miserable and caused you pain. If you choose to deny those thoughts, get an honest friend to remind you of the complaints you had about him.
6. Begin doing something that is positive for you. Take a course, a trip, or just pamper yourself at the salon, etc.
7. Build up your self-esteem again. Make a list of your assets. Tell yourself what he loses by not being in a relationship with you. After all, he just blew a great opportunity—loving you.
8. Finally, reorganize and regroup your social network. Having lots of people you can count on is good love insurance. You will never be tempted to rely solely on one person.

Chapter 6
Self-Empowerment: A Prerequisite for Healthy Sharing

Through her own choice of entering this world of contradictions, and with increasing consciousness creating
her role within herself, woman comes to the freedom
defined by Jung: "freedom of will is the ability to do
gladly that which I must do."
—FRANCES G. WICKES
The Inner World of Choice

Man sharing is a difficult concept for many women, because
the whole idea denies the kind of love absorption some
women have come to expect in relationships.

Women everywhere try so hard to maneuver a man into
caring for them with some semblance of warmth and sensitivity. Many say to me, "If only I could get him to do this or
that." "Maybe if I don't answer the phone, he'll call me more
often." "I know what I'll do; I'll let him see me with someone else, and then he will come around."

My answer to this kind of strategizing is simple: "Forget
it." Women must learn to stop organizing their behavior
around what men do or don't do. Many women who are in
dilemma about their relationships are reluctant to take this

advice; they feel that with so few available men, any is better than none. This notion, however, gives women a scent of desperation that men can smell for miles around. It also makes women extremely vulnerable in shared relationships, because they are so caught up with keeping a man that they rarely stop and consider if he's right for them in the first place. Too many women today, even after fifteen years of consuming themselves with the fight for liberation, still see a love relationship as the be-all and end-all. Women need to understand the dynamics of this trap, because it may be today's most baffling dilemma for women. We hear much talk about the "new woman," but few analysts address how uncomfortable many women still are with the vast array of options before them.

I struggle with my own life on a day-to-day basis, and the only thing new about any of this is that I never intended to be struggling by myself. I freely admit that I bought in on the dreams of most little girls—that when I grew up, if I did all the right things, the man, children, and dream house would fall into place. Even while I busied myself pursuing an education, I never imagined that I would have to support myself, pay the bills, buy the car and condo, and plan for a financially secure future. The so-called superwomen I see at many of my man-sharing workshops share the same disillusionment. They don't mind taking care of themselves, but they want a man to share the struggle with. These women find the concept of man sharing reprehensible. This is not what they worked so hard for.

I have a friend who makes more than a decent salary, and she is looking for a man with lots of money and stature to somehow save her. I am baffled, because she has all the means at her disposal to save *herself.* Such women have what I call a messiah complex, searching within each man they meet for those secret ingredients that will save them—but

from what I don't know. Unless they face themselves honestly, these women aimlessly wander the bars and byways
wondering with each "hello" if this is the man who will save
them.

The struggle for real self goes on within each woman, and
often there are two distinct personalities—independent and
dependent—raging for dominance. On the job, the modern
woman is the self-assured professional at ease with complex
decision making; yet, in her personal life, she is a weak,
submissive partner afraid to make demands for fear of losing out on this one chance for the brass ring of romance.

The emotional upheaval brought on by nonexclusive relationships can be devastating for the woman who has never
defined for herself a strong sense of self-esteem. Women
who feel powerless in relationships, especially shared relationships, are asking to be shortchanged or hurt. When sharing is forced upon them, as it usually is, these women feel
unable to control their personal space. But that is nothing
new. This woman can't give you a yes or no to an evening
bridge game until she finds out what the man in her life
wants to do. And if her man decides hang gliding is a must
activity, this woman will go with him, hold her breath, and
jump. It would never occur to her that she could play rac-
quetball with a friend while he tries to replace Evel Knievel.

I know a married woman who has allowed her husband
to decide even what she likes to eat. The fact that clams on
the half shell make her gag on sight doesn't keep her from
trying them, because he loves them so. She figures that sooner
or later he will discover her culinary tastes, but, of course,
he never does, because she never speaks up and says, "I
don't like clams. I'll have something else." Women who allow the man to call all of the shots never realize that they
will be stuck with the consequences of his choices.

In Marilyn French's book *The Women's Room,* the wife

asked her husband to tell her what he wanted her to be and she'd be it. That statement always suggested to me such a passive position for a woman. Yet many of us make that statement in various ways when dealing with a man, especially when we know he has another woman. Some women are afraid to assert themselves when sharing a man because they fear losing him to the other. Ask yourself sometimes, "How can I lose what I never had?"

When you spend time avoiding reality in a relationship, you risk not getting what you want. In fact, after a while, you risk not knowing what you want.

Many factors contribute to a woman's feeling powerless to act in her own behalf in a relationship with a man. Social rearing is perhaps the main culprit. The practices of pleasing, being responsible for others, demonstrating sensitivity are encouraged and rewarded in little girls. Females, thus, learn early to satisfy others at the sacrifice of themselves. I believe this conditioning creates adults who are uncomfortable taking care of themselves, because they have come to believe that assertion and confidence are synonymous with being selfish.

Little boys, on the other hand, are generally not burdened with the knowledge that to please others will be one of life's highest attainments. Individuation is urged and valued in male children. Self-development is a natural for most adult males.

Too often women seek intimacy with men just to sanction their own existence, while men seek validation of their self-worth in other endeavors. In other words, you are busy caring for his needs and he is busy tending to his needs, thus leaving no one looking out for that all-important person—you. Women agonize and become guilt-ridden when they seek to fulfill their needs, while men see this as their right.

If a man has more than one woman in his life, he may not see this as a great moral dilemma. In fact, one man told me, "Having a lot of women demonstrates to other men your ability to influence, control your own life, and have power." Women must learn to seek different ways to satisfy many needs. The problem is, taking action goes against everything they have been taught about what it is to be a woman.

While it would be unfair to assume that only women suffer from feelings of helplessness, it is true that women, more so than men, freely give in to these feelings and manifest them more openly. This explains why women are often so consumed with the quest of improving relationships.

A study by Jean Baker Miller in the book *Toward a New Psychology of Women* found that a woman's ability to address her own needs is related to how well she defines and feels about herself. Miller found women of all age groups expressing a common theme: They had lost the ability to value what they thought, felt, and decided. They did not experience themselves as resourceful or knowledgeable, especially when it came to dealing with the men in their lives.

Women rely so heavily on being guided by what others believe that they learn to doubt their own wisdom. Freedom and power become unfamiliar feelings. So even when the choices are apparent, women are reluctant to make them, at least not without the sanction of someone "greater than themselves."

Women in this society receive so many double messages. On the one hand, we are told to "go for it," but at the same time, we get the subtle hint that if we really get all we can out of life, the "big prize" of having a man exclusively will elude us. And true enough, many men today are extremely uncomfortable with self-actualized women who are determined to maximize their own potential despite the effects on a given relationship. In fact, women who become comfortable with their own power and worth may find themselves in a situation where a partner feels ambivalent about how this power is asserted. Sometimes he may feel relieved about your confidence; at other times, you may get the message you're becoming a "sassy bitch." Try to keep these messages in realistic perspective. You may not always get the responses from men that you expect, but you should not let this deter you from a path of individual growth and development. Remember, you must be happy with yourself before you can give pleasure to others.

Self-esteem is too often seen by women as a commodity with highly diminishing returns. Too much is not good, many of us are taught at an early age. Yet self-esteem goes to the very core of a person's ability to take full responsibility for what he or she may get in relationships that are shared. With self-esteem you may be able to keep your head above water; without it you will definitely sink under the weight of the frustrations and disappointments that will exist when you do not feel in charge. In the book *Women and Self-Esteem,* the significance of self-esteem for women is considered from many angles. "It affects the choices we make— choices about what we will do with our lives and with whom we will be involved. It affects our ability to take action to change things that need to be changed. If a woman has an insufficient amount of self-esteem, she will not be able to act in her own best interest. And if a woman has no self-esteem at all, she will become overwhelmed, immobile and eventually will give up."

Tying up the need for romantic love so inextricably with one's self-esteem is asking for trouble. It's the ultimate set-up. Census studies show that the likelihood of women living great portions of their lives alone is highly probable because of the extreme imbalance in the sex ratio as we get older. So what are we to do during those times when no significant relationship is available? Surely life must go on with a mate or without one, and this is as true at twenty-five as it is at sixty-five.

The way out of this dilemma can be scary and painful, but one which must be taken if women are to stop feeling victimized by men. Blaming men for the situations we find ourselves in does no one any good. Scapegoating men allows us the dangerous luxury of wallowing in self-pity or what I call the "woe is me" syndrome. The misery that some women wrap themselves in once they find that the man in their life is not theirs alone saps them of precious psychic energy. This time could be better utilized unraveling the whys of one's own behavior. Learning to control yourself is the ultimate power in any relationship.

Self-control frightens some women because it conjures up risks. We tend to push it aside in relationships, even when it's clearly within reach, hoping that somehow we may get a little power for ourselves without the man noticing or that perhaps he may even give us just a little. Women are like so many oppressed peoples who, through the ages, have felt that power will come to them only through association with the dominant group. We perceive that men have it all and therefore they do, but only because we believe it.

Phyllis Chesler and Emily J. Goodman, in their book, *Women, Money, and Power,* state that the whole idea of women gaining control over their own lives is a radical notion, because it is such an extreme departure from the realities of the day. "Women, of whatever class, are in trouble," they write, "if they are dependent on the income which they gain solely through a man, for the love of a man, or the pleasure of a man. . . ." Or, in the words of Dr. Carolyn R. Payton, a Washington, D.C., psychologist, "No one gives up power freely. You always have to push the oppressor off your back."

When things are going wrong with some gentleman, ask

yourself honestly, "What is the worst that could happen to me if things don't work out with him?" The answer will probably startle you. Women laugh at me when I tell them I know of no one who has died from lack of sex or even lack of a man. Certainly, we all seek to be loved, and love can be one of life's greatest pleasures, but is it really love when it is gained from total self-sacrifice?

With man sharing, it is absolutely essential that you learn to establish your own limits. You can't consume all of your energies in the pursuit of the one and only man. No woman's life depends on one man.

I wonder if most women realize the kind of power they are investing in a man when just his decision to call or not to call can send them into a maelstrom of anxiety. If we are to live truly "liberated" lives, we can't continue to live at the whim of men. When women become custodians of their own lives, they will be able to approach relationships with men with much less fear and anxiety, because men will no longer be in control of the outcome.

The agenda that I set out for women is not designed to control men, and this disappoints many women. My approach is designed to help women create strategies that will free them up to take better care of themselves in the sexual arena. To become sexually savvy, women must feel relaxed about how to get what they want out of life.

HOW TO BECOME COMFORTABLE WITH CHOICES

Women who share openly need to constantly check their feelings to be sure they are making the best choices for themselves. The more you learn to make choices and accept the outcomes, the more your sense of power and confidence will increase. Risk-taking and adventure will then seem less awesome. Becoming comfortable with choice will also reduce feelings of shame and embarrassment, because what others think will become less important.

To be able to negotiate the terms of your shared relations with men, you must forget about giving men all the power of decision. If they make all the decisions and you willingly fall in line, you have no right to complain when you are left feeling unfulfilled. I see women react like this all the time, especially when I allow men into the man-sharing workshops. Instead of focusing on the hows of building viable strategies for themselves, the women turn the meetings into grievance sessions, continually beseeching the men to tell them why they treat women as they do. When you ask men the whys of their behavior, you set yourself up by relinquishing all of the power to them. Indirectly, you are saying that men have all the answers, and if they will just give you the right ones everything will be wonderful. Little do you know, men usually will give you the answer they feel you need to hear. Historically, women have had so little power in this society, why do we give up what little we have so easily?

Dr. Payton suggests that women who adopt the "have pity on me" attitude are afraid of the repercussions of taking charge for themselves. Unconsciously, they feel that getting themselves together will mean that no man will ever want to deal with them. Women, she says, refuse to accept the fact that all choices require some risks and opt instead to remain in what they see as safe yet unsatisfying relationships. It is Dr. Payton's belief, and one that I share, that women fear the loss of an intimate relationship so much because it is only in that context that they feel comfortable having their sexual needs met.

"We don't have male prostitution," Dr. Payton observes, "so how is a woman to get her sexual needs met? If women could learn to separate their purely physical needs from romantic fantasy, they could avoid a lot of hurt and pain."

In Philadelphia, I met a forty-five-year-old physician who struck me as a woman in full control of her destiny. When she needs sex, she told me, she picks up the phone and calls her "closet lover," a man whose sexual prowess she finds fully satisfying but with whom she would never consider a longtime association. She has built up no romantic illusions about him; she enjoys him for sex and nothing more. Of course, the woman who feels she must be bowled over by love before she can enjoy sex could never compartmentalize the men in her life this way. She must romanticize every sexual encounter in order to legitimize pure sexual pleasure.

A business colleague once confided, "I simply can't live without sex, I've got to have it." I observed that she also unwittingly accepted whatever a man offered in exchange for the sex she felt she had to have. She never learned to separate sexual release from sexual fulfillment. Although she secretly wanted love, she went after sex, and then wondered why she always felt such a letdown after encounters with her lovers.

Women sometimes wince when I say, "Control over your groins will follow control over your minds." The sexual urge is a human one in need of no explanations or excuses; women must recognize and accept this fact. Romanticizing what clearly is only a sexual liaison confuses a woman's ability to take care of herself in relationships. If she views every man as a potential husband, or if she thinks not having a man is a potential disaster, she leaves herself little room in which to maneuver—and in a constant state of anxiety.

Patterns are not traits you are both with; they can be broken, but not unless you are willing to see things as they really are. Too many women repeatedly go back to the same kind of unsuccessful relationships, only to experience the same emptiness. It is critical that you periodically take a look at your patterns and what role *you* play in the outcome of your relations with the opposite sex.

Learning to uncover your love patterns is a skill that will release you from the emotional traps you may often find yourself in with men. Some observers say women attract what they need, and I believe this is true, even when what we seek is not good for us. Unresolved conflicts about familial relationships and past social experiences with men will continue to play themselves out in all of our encounters if we don't take the time to find out why we do what we do. It is no accident that some women always find themselves unhappily involved in shared relationships. If sharing is not for you, but you always seem to end up in these relationships, look at your patterns. Examine your patterns, too, if you repeatedly attract men who use and abuse you. Often, because of low self-esteem, women typecast themselves as unworthy of love and respect. Then they unconsciously seek out a man to reinforce these feelings about themselves. Women need to become emotional detectives and find out why they continually choose destructive roles. Believe me, the heartache of self-discovery is well worth the momentary anguish. This may mean getting some help from a professional therapist or counselor. Sometimes some objective guidance is all you need to begin making important behavioral changes. Of course, the therapist cannot and will not do the work for you.

A thirty-five-year-old single woman told me, "I woke up one day realizing that if you can't take control and full responsibility for yourself and stand behind all your decisions and choices, you go through life being someone else's baby doll or puppet." Unfortunately, many women choose to be puppets rather than puppeteers.

Like *power, control* is a word women shy away from, because it conjures up images of the shrewish woman who makes men cower in her presence. Control need not be a negative action. Rather, it is a positive decision about your involvement in all situations in your life. If a man you have been seeing tells you, "You're not the only woman I see, so you should see others," believe him, then decide if this arrangement fits in with your plans. You may choose to see him less frequently and only for certain activities, or you may decide you don't wish to see him at all. However, if you decide to stop seeing a man, if there is no man in your life, or if you find yourself in several "sometimey" affairs with different men, you still have the question of how to satisfy your own sexual needs.

If you share, there are always options. If you refuse, you may need to come to grips with periods of celibacy that, if used correctly, can work for you and not against you. Recently, I saw a woman on a television show explaining why she had chosen a temporary state of celibacy for herself. This pretty blonde said to an incredulous announcer that celibacy gave her some control over her personal life: She no longer flitted from one man to the next in search of sexual fulfillment.

THE POWER OF VOLUNTARY CELIBACY

Everyone needs a sexual sabbatical periodically, and none so much as those who persist in playing romance roulette and those who resist or are tired of sharing. An attractive forty-seven-year-old woman told me that after years of one shared relationship after another, she decided to drop out socially. She said that she knew when she chose celibacy that it would not be forever, but she needed a break to determine where she wanted to be in the sexual arena. She had felt pressured to participate in less than satisfactory relations with men, just so that she could have a man in her life. Clearly tired of "the endless games," as she described them, she wanted instead to feel more control over her life.

"I spent the time reading a lot of self-help books and going to lectures and workshops on growth and development for women," she said. "The first couple of weeks were the hardest, but I tried not to focus on my lack of sex. I spent a great deal of time by myself and learned to listen to my own feelings and to trust them."

After a year of celibacy, this woman resumed a full social life, but she no longer felt compelled to accept every social offer that came her way. She now dates two men when it's possible, but if a weekend comes up when neither is available, she doesn't panic and worry about having nothing to do.

A celibate period, she said, helps you learn how to relax in new relationships. It can also give you room to maneuver in old relationships. Since you establish no timetables when you meet someone new, you have time to get to know the person and decide what, if anything, you might have in common. This notion is especially helpful when you are considering sharing a man, because you can allow time to explore the benefits of a situation before leaping in.

Although celibacy frightens some women, who see it as deviant or weird behavior, when you consider that many of us will experience some periods of celibacy in our lifetimes, whether we choose it or not, it becomes less ominous.

Consider Louisa, a thirty-six-year-old public-relations executive in Los Angeles, who believes that a two-year self-imposed period of celibacy ultimately changed her whole outlook on life. After many affairs with married men and broken affairs with single men, Louisa began to feel used up. "For a couple of years I went hog wild dealing with men," she said. "I dealt with so many I lost count. The inner pain and loneliness I felt never really went away, so I just stopped all sexual activity and tried to come to grips with some of my problems." Louisa credits her experience with celibacy with her increased sense of self-confidence where men are concerned. She learned that she could survive without sex, so it was less risky to be choosy about the men she allowed in her life. She didn't feel compelled to share when she didn't want to. She ultimately met a young actor to whom she is now married, but she has no illusions about the fact that someday she may share him with another woman. "He's much younger than I and very attractive," she said, "but we have a solid relationship right now. I'm confident I can handle the future whatever it brings."

When a woman knows that she can get along for great periods of time without sex, no man can suggest that she accept crass behavior just for the pleasure of his company. Celibacy can help women discover talents and interests they had cast aside while they participated in endless manhunts. Some women may choose to devote more time to their jobs, take up an advanced degree, spend more time with their children, or simply opt for solitude.

Celibacy can be to the body what a tune-up is to an engine; it can revitalize the system and get you ready to take off again. A woman once told me that she had chosen periods of celibacy twice in her lifetime—once out of anger, once by preference. The latter was definitely the better reason. Celibacy is an uncomfortable choice if you do it because you feel you lack options.

THE PRINCIPLES OF CHOICE

Becoming comfortable with making choices in your life may take some growing into for certain women, but it can be done. It will involve a change in attitude as well as in behavior. As I have said before, sharing relationships work best when the woman involved makes the decision that this is what she wants for herself. When the man decides sharing is what he wants and tries to impose it on the woman in his life, it is always disastrous. Women of choice don't allow anyone to decide what's best for them. They enjoy decision making about their own lives and are governed only by those rules that make sense to them and for them. I believe this approach encourages a well-adjusted life, whether women choose to share men or not. It won't make your life problem-free, but the hassles will be fewer.

PRINCIPLE 1

Realize That There Are Always Many Options Available to You.

You will never feel stuck in any relationship if you believe you have options. The options may be other men, other activities, or learning to do things by yourself. Women who insist upon having only "their type" of man limit their options from the outset. It's interesting that the women who most abhor sharing are often the ones with the longest lists of what "their kind of man" must have and do. They don't realize that their requirements only limit further an already constricted pool of available men. Women who resist sharing need to be open to all kinds of men in order to increase their opportunities to find those often-elusive monogamous gentlemen. You need to be open to quality in your relationships, and not select a man simply because of his looks, job status, or age. Men come in all sizes, shapes, and colors, and you may miss someone quite wonderful just because he doesn't fit some preconceived notion you have of what a man should be.

Never allow all your leisure time to be consumed with man-focused activities. If sharing as a way of life is not for you, consider the following: take a trip by yourself, take a mechanics course so you can fix your car, or join an investment group so you can learn to use your money more wisely. The point is, create options for yourself. Then, if a particular relationship isn't going well, you won't be so anxious all of the time.

How does this relate to sharing? Suppose you are seeing someone you like quite a lot but he's not willing to give the kind of time you feel you need. Don't struggle with this as though he's your only choice. Instead, see him from a different perspective. Make him a special friend, and decide to see others.

PRINCIPLE 2

Don't Wait for Permission to Do What Is Best for You; Never Expect Sanction for the Decisions You Make.

Women who are immobilized in crazy relationships with a man often use words like *can't, should,* and *ought to.* They are stuck but can't make a decision, because they expect him to know what they want. These women can usually give you a long list of what the man should do or could do to make them happy. However, when asked what they could do for themselves, they have absolutely no idea. They will wait around for years, hoping that the man in their life will tell them what he wants from this relationship. Or some of these women will meekly work out a shared arrangement with a husband or lover only to have it fall apart when family and friends start saying, "I don't know how you can live with that. If he were mine, I would do so-and-so." You must be willing to live with the decisions you make about your life, and you can't come unglued when others challenge you. When you have developed a strong sense of self, it won't matter to you what others think as long as you know you are doing what's best for you. Women of choice could not be so if they worried about what others thought of them.

PRINCIPLE 3

Take Responsibility for Your Actions and Resist Efforts to Place Blame When Things Don't Work Out as You Had Expected. When you are truly a woman of choice, taking responsibility for your decisions and actions will become second nature to you. If you decide to share, you do so with full knowledge of the consequences. There will never be any reason to place blame for mistakes or disappointments. This is a liberating concept, because it will free you from bitterness. If you are in charge and do only what you think is best, there will never be cause for anger. One woman admitted she was feeling a little let down after a recent breakup with a man she shared with another woman. "Things didn't work out as I had hoped, but if I'm honest with myself, I did get a lot out of it while it lasted. You always have to turn a negative experience into a positive," she told me. This attitude contributes to her growth experiences.

PRINCIPLE 4

Use Power and Control Only over Yourself. Your Goal Is Self-Control, Not Control of Others.

Accepting this principle and practicing it in relationships will stop the endless worry about being victimized by a man. Women spend far too much time trying to orchestrate romances where they won't get hurt. They mistakenly believe that if they do everything a shared man wants, he will remain with them. Or worse, they feel if they keep after him all of the time, checking his whereabouts and chasing him constantly, that somehow he won't have time to see other women. And of course, women of choice know that none of this ever works. You can't control what other people do, and even if you could, they would hate you in the long run. Ask only that others be fair with you, and offer them the same in return. Give up being detectives and forget games of manipulation; they are too time-consuming and usually futile.

PRINCIPLE 5

Don't Look for Guarantees. Go Out on a Limb and Explore the Unthinkable.

Women who are happy in sharing situations rarely feel the need for guaranteed outcomes. A predictable relationship would drive them mad, and they usually make no pretense about wanting one. Traditional men who have tried to reform these women of choice have met with failure again and again. These women don't ask a man about what's next, nor do they wait for him to talk about commitments. It's not in their makeup to set deadlines for fulfillment. The "what if's" that some women wallow in are not the stuff of conversations with women of choice. They try to make a responsible decision for themselves, and if it doesn't work it just doesn't work. They realize that with human beings, few things are certain.

* * *

I believe that no woman can operate freely in a nonexclusive relationship unless she understands and accepts the above principles. When a woman believes she has no choices where men are concerned, vulnerability results and so does unnecessary heartache.

Sharing a man you care about with another woman is not easy; I would never suggest that it is. However, I do believe that very few women in this life will escape participation in such a relationship, so preparation is tantamount to survival. Women who feel powerless can't get what they need in any relationship, even if it is monogamous. If you understand the rules of the game, then you can take care of yourself. You may never want to live the nontraditional lives of some of the women described in this book, but there are lessons to be learned from these women.

The primary lesson is that power and control need not be foreign concepts for women. Even now when we find ourselves in a social milieu where many women feel left out and uncared for, there are healthy ways to interact with the opposite sex. The important fact is that these are different times in need of very different approaches, and the old way—one man to one woman—is not going to happen for everyone. There is great power in understanding and accepting reality. Letting go of fantasies allows women to make the most of those situations that present themselves. When women truly accept reality, they will feel a sense of control over their lives that will set them free.

CHAPTER 7

The People You Will Meet Along the Way

Not everybody is in the dating game in the same way. At one time or another, they may have a serious involvement with one person that takes up most of their time. They, however, enter with the attitude, "nothing lasts forever."

—ROBERT STAPLES
The World of Black Singles

THE MEN

Categorizing people is a habit I abhor, but I am succumbing now because it's important that men and women begin to recognize the types of people most inclined toward sharing. I can hear the outcry that "we are all individuals," which is true enough, but there are enough similarities in the ways some relate to the opposite sex that one is tempted to lump these individuals into types—especially those types most likely to indulge in multiple relationships. No one trait is peculiar to a single type, but behavior patterns taken together can help you single out exactly who you are dealing with. I have a favorite saying, "It's important to know the weather report, so you will be sure how to dress." The same holds true for meeting people. If you know that the person before you is a definite sharer, your responses and expectations can be managed more easily and with much less discomfort.

Following are some of the male types likely to be sharers. Being able to recognize them is not just for singles, because some ladies find themselves married to these fellows and spend a lifetime trying to figure out their inscrutable characters. For instance, if you find yourself married to a Charmer, you are in for some long, sleepless nights unless you reconcile yourself to his philandering or call it quits. So read the following with wide-eyed bemusement and see if you recognize any of the players.

Charmer

If you have ever walked into a party and been struck by the proverbial thunderbolt, more than likely you have met the ubiquitous Charmer. He's that tall, dark, and handsome character with the voice that could melt steel and whom every woman thinks she simply must have. True to character, you probably eventually will find that many women do have him, even if only a small piece. He will wine and dine you and mesmerize you with flowers and handwritten poetry. Whatever you need, he will provide it—from sweet talk to passionate sex. He will keep you on this hedonistic diet until he is sure that he has won you.

You may be tempted to resist this game of his, but the more you resist his charms the harder he will try to conquer. He's a smart cookie and knows that every red-blooded American woman is a sucker for three little words: *I love you.* So one night, over some Courvoisier in front of a raging fireplace, he will look longingly into your eyes and utter those three words that will ensure his place in your heart. At this point, you are so delighted that your search for the perfect mate is over that you relax and call all your friends to start preparing the wedding feast. But don't move too quickly—his program is just in phase one of operation.

The next phase begins as soon as he is sure you have succumbed totally to his wiles. Suddenly, phone calls come less frequently, and more and more business meetings take place at night, keeping him regrettably away from you. Frequent changes in plans replace the old eagerness that kept you on the verge of euphoria. After a few weeks or even months of these subtle changes, you probably will begin to check out some of the stories. While you are checking, you undoubtedly will stumble upon another woman or several other women. When you confront him, he will be nice but noncommittal, passing things off with, "I'm sorry things just didn't work out."

In the meantime, he has another woman deep in the throes of the passion of his phase-one operation and has no time to soothe your hurt feelings. But wait! When things start settling down with his new lovely, he will return to you, saying, "I don't know what came over me. You were the best thing that ever happened to me." If you fall for this, brace yourself for another round on the ropes and an outcome like the first time. This is a cycle the Charmer will repeat with you and numerous others. He prides himself on having many different women who will merrily collude in his program, each one thinking that with just a little patience he will change. He won't change, because it's not in him: The conquest is what he enjoys. He will change only when it is in his best interest, and who can wait for that to happen?

Hit-and-Run Man

This man is the Charmer's first cousin. His opening moves are very similar—fast, loose, and eager to please. The main difference is this man isn't willing to put in as much time wooing, he knows in the beginning that he will be moving on rather quickly. He surrounds himself with many women, because he thinks one is too time-consuming. Keeping women on a string is his forte. He will literally hit the ground running, and you may feel a bit overwhelmed by his hasty ardor. With him, pillow talk will come up right away, as time is of the essence to this man. His mottos are "Live for today" and "Live life in the fast lane." Long-range planning is definitely out of his ballpark. This guy thrives on having an assortment of women that he can call on in a hurry. He may sit at his phone and make one call after another until someone says, "Yes, you can come over tonight." He will run to her house, have a quick drink, and hurry off to bed, of course, rarely spending the night because he has no time. "Talk to you later" are the only four words that you will hear from Mr. Hit and Run.

Two-Step Lover

This frustrating guy is the classic distancer. He will leave no stone unturned as he attempts to engage you in a relationship, but any positive response from you will cause him to step back, although not away. He will hang in there, always at a safe distance. If you move in, he will move two steps backward. If you step back, after many frustrating attempts at intimacy, he will move up close. This cycle could go on forever, if your heart can stand it. The real problem with this man is that he usually is a perfectly nice fellow whose fear of commitment and intimacy keeps him in constant motion—not only in and out from you but also from one woman to another. The old motto that there is safety in numbers keeps this guy going; the more the merrier. He feels safe that he will never have to commit to anyone. You may play the game with him for a while, thinking that eventually he will come around, but he won't. The two-step is no fun when you are constantly tripping over your own feet.

Trickster

This is the cold-blooded con man who has preyed on lonely women since time began. He stalks his victims very carefully, studying their every move before he strikes. His favorites are lonely, desperate women. He always wants something from you; something you possess intrigues him—it may be something as intangible as your status in the community or professional contacts. Once he engages you, he unfolds a sob story about how he has been trying to find himself, needing only a good woman to give him a break. He will tell you half-truths. For example, he may have this blockbuster business idea that has stalled because of lack of financing and if you could just invest a few thousand, it would get him started. "Who knows? You might make a killing on this project. I would love to have you as a partner." If you have recently met this man and this kind of tale comes up, move out quickly and smartly, because more than likely you are in the hands of the Trickster.

Another familiar story sounds like this: He may be going on a job interview after many agonizing months of unemployment, and all he needs from you is your American Express card to get a new shirt and tie for the interview. His needs will be endless once you start opening your heart and your wallet. He's slick enough to have your ego soaring to the sky, and he will have put you on such a pedestal that no other man can reach you. You will wake up one morning realizing how very little you know about your new love except how much he loves sharing your things. The only good thing about him is that he won't be around very long, but his brief tenure can prove very costly. *Beware.*

El Jocko

His haunts are jogging and bike trails, health clubs and workout joints. He is so into his body and maintaining good health that his behavior borders on the obsessive-compulsive. He makes his own juices and weighs all of his food. If he gains three pounds, he will call you in a deep depression about the demise of his overall condition. He is so paranoid about germs that he runs to the sauna every day to sweat them out of his system. He does everything with compulsion and, of course, he can't focus on you, because he is totally consumed with himself. He will surround himself with lots of women because this validates his masculinity, which is rather shaky beneath all the bravado. He may brag to his buddies that he is in such good shape that he can last all night or that he can take on many women in one day, but don't believe it. This health maniac could be a real shrinking violet in the bedroom. After all, he can't let little you sap up all of his energy.

Menopausal Maynard

This poor chap is over forty years old or very close to it, and he is literally running scared. Simply, he must make many women succumb to him each day or all life will be over for him. This is the type of man who will arrive at your door with his shirt open to his navel, medallion hanging on his hairy chest, or wearing pants so tight you think he will scream. If he has started losing his hair, be prepared for some of the most innovative hairstyles you have ever seen. Even Vidal Sassoon will have nothing on this man: Menopausal Maynard will try anything to cover up his gray or the loss of hair. He lives in constant fear of heart attack, so be gentle with him if you decide to take him home. Don't worry about his latching on to you, however, unless you happen to qualify as a bona fide teen-ager; the younger the better. He needs constant adoration and attention, and if your teenybopper days are over, leave this guy alone.

Recently Divorced Ralph

This guy could well be the dating game's answer to Mean Joe Greene. He is ready to do battle with the world because one woman, his ex-wife, took him for everything he had. To guard against ever falling for a woman again, he builds walls around himself that would rival the Great Wall of China. He also tries to build a harem so that some woman will always be at his beck and call. Mean and nasty fights may crop up over little things, because he has to take his frustrations out on a woman, and you are just as good as any. Stay out of his way on the day his wife hauls him into court for more money or nonpayment of alimony, because if you happen to be in his path, you will pay for all her transgressions.

Now, all divorced men are not mean. There's another type who is so ambivalent and gun-shy about women that a nursemaid is what he really needs. If you meet a man whose divorce or separation was rather recent, my advice is to attempt friendship initially and wait to see what happens. This way you can commiserate with him without getting your feelings hurt when he can't separate you from the shrew he just left. However, if she left him, you are in real trouble. When the wife jumps ship, most men are devastated, even if the marriage was in shreds from the start. Leaving is a man's prerogative, and most men feel this way; don't be fooled. What this guy needs most of all is nurturing, and unless you feel like feeding him with a long-handled spoon, make him a buddy or an occasional movie date. You will cut down on the heartache if you don't get too close, at least until he gives some signal that he is ready for more.

The Married Man

These are the men who make up what a friend of mine calls the Sock Brigade. They have won this name because they want to be sure that they don't get dressed in such a hurry that they forget to pull on their socks. The Married Man wants no telltale sign of his cheating to get home to his wife. I have heard of all the good things that a married man can give, but I'm not convinced that his surface warmth, sensitivity, and eagerness to please you are worth the long-term hassles. The women who claim that they can handle their second-class status with this man are usually the ones who fall the hardest. And hoping for this man to leave his wife and come to you is generally pure folly. Melissa Sands writes in her book *Survival Guide for the Mistress* that, contrary to what they may tell you in the midst of passion, most men never leave their wives. Although many women live for the day when the man will leave home, most married men don't leave home because having a mistress actually helps make their marriages more bearable. They stay and tell themselves that they are "good enough husbands," because they take care of home well. Even in the few cases where a man might leave his wife, he generally ends up not wanting his mistress either. If he does happen to marry his mistress, she very often finds herself in the same position as the previous wife. However, if all you want is a good friend and a sometime lover, the Married Man may be the answer. However, be real clear on your objectives before you jump in the sack with this sweetie.

Sugar Daddy

This guy is frequently a married man who feels that the only way he can win you over is to offer you the world on a silver platter. He is the embodiment of Shirley Temple's "Goodship Lollipop." The problem is that like the Godfather, he usually makes an offer you feel you can't refuse. He may come along when the rent is overdue and the bank is ready to repossess your car. He makes it clear from the start that money is no object—if you need it, he's got it. However, with this arrangement the goodies often carry with them a high price tag, and you better decide up front if you are willing and able to pay. This man provides, but with great expectations about your availability to him, usually whenever and wherever he so chooses. If you can take having upon you once again the constraints of a child, go full speed ahead. However, if you entertain any thoughts of independence once you start taking things from Sugar Daddy, you are in for a very painful awakening. Also, he bores easily, and when he tires of you, he'll be gone, along with his goodies.

Charley the Clinger

Charley is the needy one, more than likely a loner in search of someone to whom he can attach. It's always wonderful in the beginning to meet this delightful fellow, who is more than willing to be your one and only, but with time this man and his obsession with togetherness can slowly drive you to desperation. This man will have you considering sharing just so you can get a break from him. Without many social resources of his own, he will rely on you for all of his leisure-time activities. He may even insist upon shopping with you or sitting in the waiting area while you get your hair done; that way the two of you will never be separated. He will become very much like one of your plants, which seem always in need of water. This gentleman requires solicitousness that is maddening, forcing you to begin moving away from him, which will make him cling to you even more. Stay way away from this man unless you, too, want togetherness at any cost. You also may try from the beginning to contain and keep him as a friend, but watch the encroachments carefully. He can't help himself—he simply must be attached.

The Workaholic

This guy is related to Mr. Hit and Run because he, too, has little time for wooing and courtship. His first and only love is his work, and you *always* will come in second. The self-absorption that propels this man to the forefront of his profession is the same trait that will keep you at a safe distance. Forget calling him when you want to chitchat about your day at the office or your broken-down car. He has no time for the mundane. If it's not about the latest *Dun & Bradstreet* report or a discussion of his company's annual earnings, his eyes will glaze over before you can get out your first sentence. This man may mean well and even care for you, but he will never have the time to let you know how he feels, nor will he ever make the time to really nurture a relationship. He compartmentalizes women the same way you categorize your shoes. He may have one woman who goes with him to office functions and another for quiet weekends in the country. The frustration you create for yourself in attempting to make a permanent connection with this fellow should be recycled into being satisfied with making him an occasional dinner or a movie date. Let him know you'd love to see him when he has some time, but never, ever build your social life around him.

The New "Male"

Much has been written lately about the new American male. He's a consummate cook, a sensitive lover and friend, a ready helpmate, and a professional confidant. What is generally left out when women discuss this so-called sensitive creature is that he is utterly frightened to death of commitment. In fact, he usually will have a master plan in his head about how a relationship should proceed from step to step: Each move closer to a long-term involvement will make this man shy away or simply take flight. He's the highly intelligent gentleman who espouses all the right words about women's equality and male liberation. He might even accompany you to ERA rallies and regale you with his views of what husbands and fathers should be in this new day. Look critically beneath this guy's evident grace with the new order to see how much of it he really believes. His talk about marriage and children may be a ploy to sustain your interest. He likes to make his women into buddies, because this is safe. He may have a skiing buddy, another for antique shopping, and still another for wanton sex. He may even settle on one who will reign for only a brief time—until she starts talking about commitment. However, if you are not looking for long-term commitment, this guy can make a great companion.

While my examination of male types may seem to cover only those men so neurotic no one would want to date them, let alone share them, be assured that these characters really do exist in many disguises. You may know them under other names, like playboys, swingers, and Don Juans, but whatever their names, their stings can still be unpleasant, if you don't recognize them from the start.

THE WOMEN

For obvious reasons, there are not as many types of women as there are men. Women still resist multiple relationships, but there are several types of women for whom sharing is the only way. Then there are a few other types who always find themselves in sharing situations, even though they claim to have little interest in participating.

Liberated Lilly

Lilly's goal in life is to be independent and answer to no one. She's the "take charge" type who even tries to organize the lives of her friends. She's a perfectly driven individual who evaluates men based only on what they can add to her existence. She has no time to cater to anyone, especially not a man. Her answering machine is always on, because she refuses to spend a night at home: The world might pass her by if she stopped for just one moment. Sharing men with other women means nothing to her, because the men usually mean little to her. She enjoys them for the moment, and then moves on. If a man starts driving by houses with FOR SALE signs on them, suggesting that they might make a nice twosome, this woman runs for cover immediately. She's on her way to the top, and no man is going to tie her down.

Fabulous Fanny

Fanny is totally into herself. She spends enormous amounts of money and time on keeping her body and face up to perfection. You will never see her without makeup, with chipped nail polish, or a stocking with a run. These sins are unconscionable to Fanny, who must always look perfect. Fanny has turned flirtation into an art form. She knows what to wear to make men weak, and she may practice how to tilt her head or flash her eyes to get just the right effect.

She has many men—the more the merrier—and her biggest concern in life is how to coordinate all of the men who adore her. Office mates are bombarded with stories about men who will die if they can't have her, and Fanny firmly believes the stories she tells. After all, it wouldn't occur to her that some man wouldn't give his all for just a moment with her. However, Fanny is interested in engaging a man only for the moment. She wants no long-term commitments.

Cinderella Cindy

Cindy spends most of her time fantasizing about the perfect man who is going to come along and take her to never-never land. She clips pictures of wedding dresses from *Bride's* magazine and has her hope chest full of exquisite linens and lingerie. In her mind, all she has to do is put herself in the right situations, and the man of her dreams will materialize. She surrounds herself with lots of men because the greater the numbers, the greater her chances of meeting the perfect one. Maximizing her opportunities is the rule that guides her. She sizes up men like one would fruit in a basket. If one doesn't look quite right, she tosses him away, so she can continue with her search. She doesn't want to lose any time on the wrong man, so she just keeps them coming. You would never get her to admit it, but there's something about this endless search that she enjoys. Finding Mr. Right is often just talk to disguise her real pleasure in the numbers of men she can engage over a period of time.

Panicked Polly

Polly is Cindy's older sister. She's been on the social circuit for many years and has become scared that the right man still has eluded her grasp. Polly is obsessed with having a certain kind of man, so she continually surrounds herself with as many men as possible. If a man seems like a good prospect, she holds on for dear life. If he says he must have other women, it's okay with her as long as he continues to afford her just a little of his time. She may brood about sharing him with others, but she has no intentions of rocking the boat. He might leave her, and she doesn't know what to do with herself without a man. Polly can keep up this routine for years, as long as the man gives her a little hope that eventually he will give up all others for her.

Bored Betsy

Bored Betsy has been married for several years and has discovered that passion and romance do indeed fade after many years. Her husband may be dutiful as husbands go, but she wants a little more excitement out of life. She often has wondered if her husband cheats on her, but she has been reluctant to step outside of the marriage because of what others would say if she got caught. Betsy may spend a great deal of time fantasizing about other men, and one day a particular man may make an extramarital fling too tempting to pass up. Cautiously, Betsy may give in to the charms of this other man, but all the while she struggles to keep her emotional balance. She doesn't want to fall in love; she just wants a little fun.

Daisy Dilemma

Daisy wants a relationship this week, but next week she's not so sure. She's totally dependent on a man once she's in a relationship, but she claims to hate this dependency she feels. She probably has never really been on her own, and even if she appears to be independent, she usually isn't. She says she would never share a man, but finds herself in shared relationships all the time. Each time she discovers this, she vows she will get out of the situation. However, she deliberates back and forth while she continues to hope the man will commit to her alone.

Leaving a relationship scares her to death, because she can't imagine making decisions without a man to guide her. She may even see several men whom she cares little about, and calls them into service only when no man is around. Her dilemma is that she just can't make up her mind, because she is used to having others make decisions for her and take care of her.

LEARNING THE LANGUAGE

The first step in unraveling the mysterious world of sharers is to learn their language or at least how to decode it. Men seem to have had a headstart in the mechanics of language manipulation. Generally, *manspeak,* a word coined by Erica Abeel in her book *I'll Call You Tomorrow: and Other Lies Between Men and Women,* totally mystifies and confuses women, as it is meant to do. These days a woman can't often get a straight answer for a coffee date. The game of "dodge" is alive and well, especially for men intent on having many ladies. Let's take a look at a typical male comment after an evening out with a new lady.

"Nice evening, you're really okay people. Let's get together again soon. I'll give you a call."

Now, he may call you in a few days or weeks, but the chances are not very good. "Okay people" is very impersonal, right? And "I'll call you" doesn't tell you when. It could be tomorrow, next year, or never. The point is that the comment is wrapped in vagueness that is designed to keep him off the hook and you off balance. Forget direct answers to direct questions. Listen to this exchange after a man and woman have had a few dates.

"Hi, why don't we get together Friday night?" she asks.

"Well . . . I don't know. I have to check this out. I may have to go out of town, and I have a class I might have to study for. Let me get back to you," he says as he successfully wiggles out of giving a direct answer.

She can wait around for that call if she wants to, but I wouldn't place any bets on these two getting together on Friday night.

Another familiar conversation comes when a woman who wants a commitment tries to find out where she stands in a relationship. This concern probably comes toward the end of the first two or three months of dating.

"We've been seeing quite a bit of each other," she says demurely. "Where are we going with this relationship?"

"I enjoy you; you enjoy me," he answers defensively. "Let's leave it at that for now, and see what happens."

Another couple discuss why there has been no contact for several weeks. She believes it's because he's seeing someone else.

"Hi, it's been a long time since we've talked," she says.

"Well . . . I guess one activity led to another and I got busy," he says.

"Are you seeing someone else?"

"I see lots of people; I'm a gregarious guy."

Neither of the above women got any concrete information after questioning their male friends.

A woman I met at a workshop in Denver, Colorado, told me she was perplexed by her boyfriend's need to feed her half-truths. She knew she was sharing him, but didn't understand why he still couldn't level with her. She was a lady who liked to know what was going on around her. When her boyfriend, with whom she lived, would disappear over long, extended periods, he'd be able to give only vague and unsatisfactory explanations of his whereabouts.

She said, "I thought we had an open, honest relationship and that we were both consenting adults. I couldn't figure out why he would respond to me so generally. I asked, 'Where do you go all day?' He said, 'Out taking care of business.' Then I'd ask, 'What about the evening hours?' He'd say, 'Well, I got caught up in a poker game at a local pub and lost track of the time.' " This type of dialogue went on for months, with her frustrations growing by the day. When she told him about her need for the truth when he was going to be away for extended periods, he saw this as a woman's insecure need to check up on him.

This lady finally realized that a mature relationship was not possible with this guy, and she just gave up asking questions. Not asking too many questions is usually best, because most women already know the answers to the questions anyway. Women more so than men get stymied around semantics, often because they don't want to understand the truth.

However, women are more adept than men at the coy games of subterfuge. Some will lead a man on for weeks, only to explode when he finally makes advances toward her. Somehow he is supposed to know that she was just flirting and had no interest in following through. Women are also good at dropping hints about what they want from a man, and feel generally misunderstood when he doesn't seem to catch on. Men often say that they don't know what women want, and often they truly don't, because the lady in question has never stated her desires clearly.

Another prevalent sharing maneuver is the "I love you" game. Men know the power in these three little words, and they won't hesitate to use them if they feel a woman needs them. Women, on the other hand, upon hearing these words, usually take them very seriously and may indeed begin looking at the relationship differently. In deciphering whether a person truly loves you, forget about how often he says he does. A better way to judge is to watch how you are treated. If you are treated in a loving and concerned manner, you're in business. Otherwise, attribute the "I love you's" to a serious case of pure and simple lust.

These days it's also difficult to figure out what "friend" means in terms of relationships. This loose term usually lets someone off the hook of actually explaining the true nature of a relationship. A man and woman may very well be friends, but this fact doesn't preclude the possibility that they may also have sex from time to time. People often get confused with this concept, thinking that if a woman or man is a friend that he or she is only a buddy and nothing more. Of course, often nothing could be further from the truth.

It's easy for people who share to diffuse emotional intensity and play word games because they generally don't make an emotional investment in these exchanges. Their goal is to keep things running smoothly with as few hassles as possible.

WHY THE GAMES ARE SO PREVALENT

Some men just aren't comfortable in one-on-one relationships; they find safety in numbers. Numbers give them protection from commitment, emotional involvement, and vulnerability. To some men, being close is often synonymous with entrapment. Women, too, experience anxiety about the intimacy that can come from committed relationships. They also may create situations where emotional connection is kept at a minimum. But rather than fearing entrapment, women generally fear the loss of attachment: They don't allow themselves to become involved so they will never have to experience the anxiety of being left or abandoned. The fear of commitment and vulnerability is not the sole province of either sex.

A close male friend once described to me the awesome "sinking" feeling he experienced whenever he found himself falling in love with a woman. "It was like being totally engulfed in her—you know, like being completely out of control." He compared it to being a three-year-old and having a six-foot mother in charge of your feelings. Whenever he felt he was falling in love, he ran to the next safest place—the arms of another woman. So while women fantasized and romanticized about the trappings of love, this man, like so many others, saw "love" as a threatening situation, one he was not anxious to replicate.

This fear of dependency has an overwhelming effect on the male's behavior. It's a double bind, according to Herb Goldberg in his book *The New Male: From Self-Destruction to Self-Care.* Men need women desperately, but they fear the vulnerability that comes with the need.

"His relationship with his woman is suffocated by the heavy weight of his dependency. If she abandons him, his emo-

125

tional lifeline will have been cut," Goldberg writes. "At the same time, he never clearly defines what it is that he needs or wants from her. He is regretfully tied to her from cradle to grave." In some ways, men both need this dependency and resent it at the same time.

Dr. Earl T. Braxton, a psychologist whose practice in Pittsburgh includes extensive work with young men, says that the fear of dependency is "one reason men don't readily buy in on monogamy." A man may feel he lessens his chances of "being locked in if he keeps a lot of strings out there." In addition, holding back emotionally is culturally linked to the whole concept of what it is to be a man in this society, Dr. Braxton explains. "For many a man, going to bed with a woman is a commitment for the moment, nothing more. They don't have their hearts in every bed."

Commitment for the moment simplifies life for the average male and at the same time throws the traditionally monogamous woman into emotional turnabouts that contradict all the romantic tenets she's been conditioned to believe. She wants a warm, sensitive man to care for her and only her, while he wants a warm, sensitive lady who understands that "he's got to be a man."

I believe that few men have built the emotional structure for handling modern women, even women who are willing to share them with others. Many men are telling the truth when they admit confusion about how to treat us and react to us. It took years to set up the rules our moms and dads lived by, and it will take a few more years of groping and hiding before any new rules find a consensus. Also, women send men conflicting signals. Some want it both ways—to have a "main" person but also to have options to share when it's convenient. These double messages assist men who are reluctant to practice fidelity and make it easy for them not to feel guilty.

Both sexes need clarity in communication. But we also need to remember we are in transition. We are redefining what relationships should be at a time when it's clear that infidelity is on the rise. In the meantime, frustration and confusion continue, encouraging all kinds of sharing relationships. But for women who choose to act rather than bemoan their fate, there's hope. In every social era there's always the possibility for fulfillment, no matter how bad things may seem on the surface. Again, keeping in touch with reality and not living in the past are the best guidelines for survival.

CHAPTER 8

Making It Work

The Victorian person sought to have love without falling into sex. The modern person seeks to have sex
without falling into love.
> —ROLLO MAY
> *Love and Will*

For those who decide to embark upon a quasi-polygamous
arrangement, the struggle is constant. Few people openly
acknowledge their participation in multiple relationships, so
if you are looking for rules or guidelines, you probably won't
find many. Men may secretly discuss among themselves how
they manage the various women in their lives, and women
may do the same thing behind closed doors. Still, no hand-
book exists for easy reference; the uninitiated must grope
for a way to make it work. However, looking at a few ex-
amples is often helpful. A closer examination of a few shared
arrangements may determine some common denominators.

WHEN COMMITMENT IS NOT AN ISSUE

One of the reasons that sharing seems to work for couples is that it reduces the anxiety and pressures that build up in relationships around the issue of commitment. Men and women who elect to share have an open contract with each other based on a particular activity or need. Mature couples, soon after they meet and decide that they want to see more of each other, will openly discuss on what basis they will continue to relate. They may agree to see each other every other week, once a month, or whenever the mood strikes. In these situations, neither person agonizes over when or if the other is ever going to get around to discussing the happily-ever-afters. Both can relax and enjoy whatever has brought them together in the first place.

For example, a young woman named Anna met a man at a friend's house. She knew he saw several other women, but also enjoyed his company so much that she agonized over whether she should also see him from time to time. This was a difficult decision for her initially, because she had always considered herself a "one man at a time woman." One evening, they met for drinks, and he seemed more than willing to help her examine her uncertainties about him and the possibilities of a workable relationship.

"I told him I was tired of playing all of the mating games," she said. "I travel a lot and don't have much time at home. When I'm in town, though, sometimes I would like a man to do things with. He told me that he, too, was very busy with grad school and a part-time job but would love to see me when we could both find some free time."

After a few months, Anna said that she was feeling very comfortable with this new situation. *Relaxed* was the word she used quite frequently to describe her feelings about this new relationship. "I saw a man for nearly two years before this new guy and was always upset over something or another. We spent a great deal of time together, and I truly believed that one day we would marry. He never could quite go that far, because he was content with the way things were. He was committed to me, but only to what we had then. He was clear that he needed no more."

In retrospect, Anna said, she isn't sure that a marriage with her former lover would have been a good idea anyway. She simply had felt that after a certain amount of time two people should either marry or stop seeing each other. Why she felt this way, she didn't know, because marriage was never a compelling issue for her—her career always came first.

"I don't have the time or energy to chase after people and beg for this and that," she said. "With my new friend, we respect each other's privacy and have wonderful times together. He is very good to me when he's with me, and that's really all I want."

While Anna was able to resolve her problems about commitment, there are some couples in obviously shared situations who continue to struggle with the same issue. Some refuse to accept the notion of a "commitment of sorts" that comes without a rigid list of expectations. That is the case with the following story about a triangle that continually threatens to break apart.

"THREE'S COMPANY"

Cal, a forty-four-year-old male from Nebraska, divorced for about ten years, told me, "Monogamy was never part of my makeup. I have always liked a variety of sexual partners, even when I was married." A busy museum curator, Cal has spent quite a bit of time creating sexual situations that suit his taste for nonexclusivity. We sat down one afternoon as he anxiously described his living situation to me. As his story unraveled, all I could think of was the once-popular television show *Three's Company*.

About four years ago, Cal met a woman named Kate, who connected with him almost immediately. They related well intellectually and physically and began to spend a great deal of time together. After a while, the glow of new love began to fade, and Cal and Kate decided to "just be friends." In the meantime, Cal met another woman, named Tracey, who attracted him erotically and emotionally, and he asked her to move in with him. Tracey moved in and things worked well for a time, until she realized that Kate was in the picture again. Cal told me he got tired of lying to Tracey about Kate and decided to let everything out in the open, hoping that Tracey and Kate would accept the fact that he cared for both of them, however differently.

Feeling somewhat guilty—he expected both women to explode upon their discovery of each other's importance in his life—he told me that while he likes Tracey, he thinks he truly loves Kate, who he describes as his "soul mate." He says his ideal goal would be to have the women meet each other and work out their feelings, and, perhaps, eventually become like sisters. His goal, however, seemed rather naive after I had spoken with both of the women.

Tracey, the younger of the two women, was visibly distraught when Cal told her how he felt about Kate. "It's so hard, mainly because he refuses to lie to me. I know when he's going to be with her, and this really hurts. I went away one long weekend, knowing he was going to be with Kate. I called on Sunday and told him I would be back earlier than expected and would prepare something special for dinner. He wasted no time telling me that he intended to spend the rest of the weekend doing what he was doing and that I could come back early if I wished. The fact that he wouldn't change his plans really hurt me," she said, beginning to cry. "I can't handle all of this honesty, but I don't want the lies either. I don't think I can stick this out much longer."

Tracey said that over the previous few months her feelings had wavered in this combination—*pain, hurt,* then a breathing space when she thinks things will work out—only to experience the cycle again—*pain, hurt.* Kate, on the other hand, said that she "experienced the hurt years ago when I first discovered that Cal slept with other women. I would walk in the neighborhood and see his car parked at this other woman's house. I knew he spent the night with her, and when I would ask him, he would always tell me yes, he was sleeping with this lady. I'd then hang up the phone, feeling hurt and dejected. But that stuff is behind me now.

"There are many traits about Cal that I cherish," Kate continued. "I really do need him in my life right now. He has been so supportive while I've been working on my doctoral dissertation. One night, I woke up in a panic and called him, and he came right over. I know I can count on him this way, even though I can't count on him not to see other women."

Kate said calmly that now that she knows he is living with someone (Kate eventually met Tracey at a local fair), she has decided to treat him like a married man. "That means no more spending the night, and I don't call his house anymore. I think I'm beginning to wean myself from him, but I don't have time now to run the streets looking for men, so he'll satisfy me for the time being."

The arrangement among these three left each with parts of a relationship he or she wanted to salvage for some reason. Tracey called me shortly after our first talk to tell me she was pregnant, and I sensed she thought this might be her trump card. Cal called me, too, nervously telling me about the pregnancy and openly worrying about Kate's reaction to this latest twist in their saga. Although he told me that Kate took it very well, he clearly misread her signal. He thought her calm denoted acceptance when, in fact, it was a mask for what could easily be described as indifference to his problems with this other woman. Kate typifies many of the "older" women I meet who sometimes, especially in their late thirties, decide to make what could be a bad situation a workable positive one. While she decided to stay in this sharing situation, I got the impression that regardless of what Cal did or wanted, the terms of her involvement with him would be Kate's and Kate's alone.

Today, Cal is still involved with both women. Tracey eventually suffered a miscarriage, but still desperately wants to have a child with Cal. Cal sees her more often, especially since Kate has begun teaching and spends more time concentrating on her career. Sharing is an accepted alternative that Kate is dealing with only when it is convenient for her. She no longer waits for Cal to call the shots.

The women who handle man sharing best most often have attitudes similar to Kate's. They get from a man what is possible for a particular time period, and worry little about his arrangements with other women. They understand life offers no guarantees, and that it's what you make it. Another person I met shared a similar philosophy.

HOW ONE WOMAN MADE IT WORK

Penny, a forty-one-year-old brunet divorcée and a professor at a leading Eastern university, is a woman who believes that it's her inherent right to seek satisfaction and never hesitates to examine the unorthodox ways of getting it.

"I dated Bob, a married man, for years, and it was wonderful," Penny says with a gleam in her eyes. "The funny thing about this is that eventually he divorced his wife to marry me, and believe me, the relationship was a much better one when he was married to someone else. Then all I had to do was focus on how to get his sole attention. My daily thoughts concerned having more time with him and my needs for an escort to all the public affairs I liked to attend. When we married, he tried to gain the control over me that he had always had over his previous wife. She was the mother, the wife, the day-care provider, the suburbanite who gave him all the support he needed to get his professional career going. While he was married to her, he even had his own phone at home where I could reach him. His wife and kids weren't allowed to answer this phone, so that tells you the kind of control he exercised over the home. I believed he was intrigued by me, because he couldn't control me in this way."

Penny outlined the events surrounding Bob's wife's ultimate discovery of their relationship. She also explained her own realization that Bob still intended to see other women— some of whom confronted Penny with the information. It was this revelation that eventually convinced Penny that dependence on one man was not for her—whether he be husband, lover, or friend.

"When we were together before we married, our concentration was on satisfying us," she says. "All we talked about was how in love we were and how much we wanted to be together, but during his trials and tribulations with his divorce, I started drifting more and more into the details of his life—his children and his parents. All of this made me feel resentful, because I had become very selfish about our relationship. To assuage my growing hostility, I began to pursue other interests and became less involved on a day-to-day basis with the relationship."

I asked if this increase in outside involvement meant other men, and Penny replied, "I had a father and a brother who were womanizers, and growing up, I watched them and decided, at a very early age, that women should have the same opportunities that men do for sexual freedom. I have always had close friends who were men, even if we weren't sexually involved, so I never can say that I restricted my access to other men under any circumstances.

"I had been married before and was very much in love with my first husband but never really trusted him. I thought we had a pretty good sex life until I met Bob, who exposed me to a kind of sex I had never had before. Here I was in my late twenties, and this man had to teach me about sexual pleasure. I would call him an expert on the female anatomy. There were absolutely no prohibitions in our lovemaking. Nothing was off limits."

She credits Bob with a sexual renaissance that has made her, some years after their divorce, very intolerant of men who cannot satisfy or understand her sexual needs. She feels that women need to view their sexual needs separate and apart from other emotional requirements they might have for a long-term relationship. While she recognizes the value of the pleasures that result when sex and love intermingle, she has no illusions that for her every encounter will be a romantic one.

"I am **very** involved with my career right now and have little time to look for men, so I tend to go back to those men I know who can guarantee me good sex. This is true with my 'secret friend,'" she says. "Quite frankly, this man, who happens to be a sanitation worker, is not anyone I would want to take out in public, but I know right now if I picked up the phone and called him that I could go to his house, strip down, and have wonderful sex. It's okay, because we both recognize that sex is the foundation and the end-all for us, nothing else. I think every woman should have someone like this who can satisfy her when she is not seriously involved with anyone."

This experience with her secret lover illustrates Penny's ability to separate the erotic from the emotional. She and her ex-husband Bob are close friends still and often enjoy exquisite sex, but she says she has no need to have him again as a daily presence in her life.

Asked about monogamy, Penny hedges. She believes in marriage, because she feels that a commitment to marriage might improve the survival statistics of American families. However, she admits that even if she married again, she probably would always have a lover on the side.

Penny's behavior is perhaps more understandable in the context of her childhood. She vividly remembers growing up in a household dominated by her father and brother "who pretty much had their way with women." She vowed at an early age that she would never allow any man to control her in the way she saw the men in her family manipulate the women in their lives.

"I'm very much in love now with a man who's much younger than I," she says. "I truly adore him, but I don't know that I could handle that kind of emotional intensity every day. Having a lover kind of defuses that intensity, and I'm not sure I could do without some breaks from the every day-ness of marriage."

In relating her story to me, Penny makes it clear that she never asks what others think of her life-style. "Women will never have any power in relationships if they ask for this and that. You just have to go out and do what is best for you. I protect my daughter from the knowledge of what I do and who I see. I don't expose her to some of the men in my life, because I don't personally believe that children can handle seeing their mothers with several different men.

But the bottom line for me is that I'm responsible for my own satisfaction and I work it out the best way I can."

While Penny's approach might seem extreme, I do believe that from her example women can develop successful nontraditional ways of relating to men. For example, Penny shared with me some of her guidelines for relating to men. Sharing really works for her for several reasons. First, time management is quite important; she doesn't like or have time for "hit and miss" sex. She manages her time well so she can be available for a quality period of time with a man. "If you're juggling," she says, "you don't want to be interrupted by phone calls, visitors, and other activities."

Second, Penny always makes an emotional separation between a sexual relationship and a love affair. But, she notes, it must always be a friendship for her if it's to last very long. Penny also is careful about how she selects the men she sees. They must be mature and experienced, or she risks being seen as a whore. "Men," she says, "may enjoy your being comfortable with your own sexuality, but they don't want this flaunted at them." Penny demands to be pleased, but also feels it's important to please others. She is comfortable being the aggressor in the relationship; it doesn't matter to her who approaches whom.

WHAT ABOUT MARRIED WOMEN?

Some married women today are grappling with the same issues as single women. "What do I do when he decides to see others?" Carmela, a thirty-four-year-old woman from San José, California, told me that she left her husband because he was cheating, only to go "out there" and find that "every man I met cheated in his own way." After two years of the single life, she returned to her husband with a decidedly different view of marriage and monogamy.

"Each man I encountered ultimately wanted to share me. I found that nothing had been avoided by leaving my husband. I returned, determined to make sharing manageable for me. Sharing is sharing, and I might as well do it with my husband, rather than take a chance with someone new. This was not an easy decision to come to. I thought about all the positive aspects of the marriage and decided what I would need to remain in the marriage," Carmela said.

"I didn't want the other women openly presented to me; I needed time, affection, and support. And finally, I wanted the same options as my husband, to see other people," she continued.

These two people know that each sees others. They are unique because they chose not to be deceitful. It wasn't an easy arrangement to make, but they decided it was better than lying and fighting for the truth. Many of you will not want this kind of arrangement, but for those who are considering it, view it as Carmela did—a way to see that her needs as well as her husband's were met.

I talked with Carmela several months after our interview, and she believed the marriage was still developing positively. They were spending more intimate time with each other, less so with others.

Another married woman told me that she participated in nonexclusive relations because it was practical for her and made it possible for her to have the kind of life-style she needed. Her decision to share was voluntary, and not based upon information that her husband was sharing.

Sylvia, a forty-six-year-old married singer from New Jersey, believes women must be practical and logical when it comes to love. Married faithfully to the same man for eighteen years, she had recently met a wealthy man who was also married. Sylvia had had no plans to have an affair, but a lack of finances due to her husband's occupation had made the marriage confining for her. Sylvia's husband is a struggling composer who remains unemployed so that he can write his music.

The married man seemed interesting to her because he wanted companionship, communication, and good, loving fun without commitment. Sylvia wanted professional connections and financial security and no commitment. She wanted material possessions her husband could never provide. She told me, "It's the greatest thing that could have happened to me. My husband is a great lover, and my lover is a great provider."

Sylvia has rationalized the situation to the point that she doesn't perceive it as sharing. Although her husband is subconsciously aware of where their extra money comes from, he hasn't confronted her because he doesn't want to rock the boat or have to seek traditional employment. Sylvia says, "It's a business arrangement, that's all." She believes that women need to stop expecting more from love situations than the relationship can obviously offer: If you can't leave an awkward situation, you should make the best decisions you can about the alternatives you have at hand. As far as Sylvia is concerned, everyone involved is content. She would never threaten her lover's marriage, nor would she leave her own husband for her lover.

It's apparent from the experiences of these women that those who coped best with sharing didn't feel that it had been imposed upon them. They knew they weren't the only women in their men's lives, but they stayed, nonetheless, because something they needed was being provided by the relationship. However, it's also true that older, more experienced women have better coping skills. That is not to say that a fifty-year-old woman married for twenty-five years to the same man won't be in the same dilemma about sharing that a twenty-one-year-old new bride will be. In general, though, I believe women who are past childbearing age have a better chance of making sharing work for them. It's extremely difficult for some younger women who desperately want children to handle the fact that the man they want is never going to commit to them solely.

The married women discussed in this chapter obviously feel comfortable with their choice to share. Yet, they often seemed to be searching for an easy solution to a dysfunctional marriage. These women are not typical in their attitudes toward sharing. They are, in fact, unique in their views. In my counseling practice, I rarely encounter married women who openly accept sharing. They usually are seeking ways to determine if their man is sharing. They also want to know how to manage the rage and disappointment that they feel when they make such a discovery.

It is not my job to suggest that my clients share; it is my job to accept where they are emotionally on this issue and to assist them in gaining control of their emotions. Then they can decide whether to work out the conflicts in their marriage, terminate the relationship, or accept that sharing will exist in their present situation.

Each of the preceding women who managed to share a man without emotional trauma was firmly footed in reality; this was critical. Tracey, the young woman in the second case study, was clearly not doing very well because she couldn't handle reality. She thought getting pregnant would make her man commit and, of course, it didn't. She will continue to be unhappy until she opens her eyes to what she really wants and then decides how best to get it. Fantasies can be a woman's worst enemy, especially when her life is organized around them. Conflicts around ethics and values can also trip up a woman who rushes into a sharing relationship before she has sorted out her innermost feelings about the practice. Too many women who are sharing a man have, at the same time, this little "inner voice" telling them that what they're doing is bad and unwholesome.

ETHICS AND VALUES: WHAT MAKES SHARING A STRUGGLE

Sharing men was a notion my Grandma would never have discussed, nor would she have considered multiple relations for herself. I'm sure she knew of men who slipped out on their wives occasionally and still others who had "some hussy," as women who dated married men were called, they kept across town, but such goings-on would never have been the fodder of family conversation. Grandma's thinking probably followed these lines: "Men just have to do these things, and nice women shouldn't concern themselves with them." Her job was to take care of the home and family, and why worry about what Granddad might do on the way home as long as he brought the groceries home with him.

Many modern women still subscribe to Grandma's values, even while their behavior in the sexual arena might suggest otherwise. Women often deny the existence of sharing because it's so in conflict with the values of their grandmothers and even their mothers. The concept causes a struggle, because open acceptance of sharing as a reality or participation in a shared relationship means that they have to give up the values of yesteryear. And for some women, breaking with the past is traumatic and a great cause for guilt.

I interviewed a spunky seventy-eight-year-old widow named Katherine who acknowledged concern about her granddaughter's penchant for going from one relationship to another without any commitments. When I spoke with her granddaughter, although she never admitted it to me, she was obviously in conflict: Her grandmother's opinion of her "many lovers" had had some affect on how she ultimately felt about it herself. She often wondered if what she was doing was wrong.

Katherine minced no words in saying that she is glad she was brought up in an era of limits on moral freedoms. "Some of these men today I wouldn't have," she said unabashedly. "They're lousy, because women have spoiled them." She said that she knew of a situation where a man cheated on his wife with one of her best friends for years. "Then he got sick, and now he's holding on to his wife for dear life. I wouldn't have anything to do with a man like that," she said.

Sex and *love* are words that Katherine uses sparingly. "What is love?" she mused. "It's respect and enjoying being together." She was quite clear that love had little to do with "jumping in and out of bed with this man and the next."

Even some women of choice have told me recently that they tire sometimes of going from one bed to the next. In fact, one writer has described this as the fast-food variety of sex. To women who have tired of musical beds, sharing sounds too much like what they have been experiencing unhappily for some time. They look at me wearily and admit they want no more of it. Sharing, however, doesn't mean that a woman has to run from one man to the next. If she has mastered some control over her life, sharing will mean only that a woman sees men who please her when she finds it desirable. This could mean that a woman sees two men or more, or she may see one man who sees others from time to time. What's important is that each individual is treated with respect and consideration. When viewed in a less erotic context, I think sharing becomes less threatening and more manageable in terms of value systems.

Values aren't the only obstacles to making sharing work. Religion also is a powerful deterrent. Premarital and extramarital sex are still frowned upon by most of the major world religions, so women who want to share and practice their religion have an obvious and often insurmountable barrier to get around.

There are no easy solutions to any of these conflicts about sharing. One thing is certain, making a shared relationship work will be a constant struggle. Clearly, it's not a choice for everyone. However, rational people know that making any relationship work—even a monogamous one—is hard work.

CHAPTER 9

The Hazards of
Man Sharing

Live as if everything you will do will eventually be known.

—HUGH PRATHER

The words *man sharing* conjure up images of intensely erotic fun and games for the man. However, when women elect to share several men, the idea is usually seen as deviant. Forget all that you have read and heard about any new morality, because the old adage "The more things change the more they stay the same" has never been truer than in human sexuality. American men still expect women to be exclusive. A man may give you much bravado about the importance of "doing your own thing," but wait until he finds out that you have taken him at his word. Hell hath no fury like a man who finds out he's just one of the boys!

In addition to the disapproval of men, women who decide to juggle pleasure will also incur the wrath of some of their more conservative sisters. "How could she do it?" "She will never get a man the way she carries on." This is just a sampling of the quips that will be exchanged among some of your women friends when they learn about Tom, Dick, *and* Harry. The point is, if having people look askance bothers you, forget about seeing several men. It won't work for you if you need special sanction, because sanction for your behavior is something you may never get.

The strong reactions I received after I coined the term *man sharing* are typical of the strong emotions elicited by the notion of women enjoying multiple sexual relationships. Hostility was obvious, but it was greater from women than from men. I received hate mail from women who suggested that I was setting up other women to be used and abused, and giving their men the "red light" to go share. And men approached me with a sly gleam in their eyes and "come hither" looks. Some men complimented me for helping women accept reality, while others saw me as a swinger they'd like to conquer.

The popular misconception of sharing is that when men share, they're sowing their oats, but when women engage in sharing, they're being victims or promiscuous. Expect little support from other women if you are open about the fact that you have more than one man in your life. Expect ridicule and hints of seduction from men once they find out that you are open to sharing. "Nice girls do" is not the American way, and won't be for some time. Regardless of how many bills legislatures might pass on equal rights for women, or how much we may feel liberated, society's rules and legal rights are still basically written by men and for men.

The "bad girl" stigma is one that women who share willingly say they experience most often. One woman used the word *cheap* when she described her feelings about being intimate with more than one man. Obviously, the backlash of the old double standard is still very much in force today. The mental tape of ought's and should's that comes from out of the past too often makes women feel guilty, especially after several sexual trysts with different men over a short period of time. Good little girls don't do that sort of thing, so women work themselves over mentally for transgressions that are more imagined than real. This "bad girl" image stirs up the guilt feelings, and guilt is one of society's most effective internal controls of women. It keeps us on the straight and narrow, towing the traditional mark. We punish ourselves with guilt when we break society's rules, and then we refuse to question how well some of these rules serve us as women. Women need to ask themselves, "Why should I feel badly about seeking fulfillment for myself?" Depending upon your answer, sharing may not be for you. Examine some of the hazards of sharing to see if they apply to you.

GUILT

Women with multiple sexual partners may feel guilty about what they are doing. Some women may even feel the need to start confessing to the men in their lives about others they may see. They feel, however mistakenly, that confession will relieve the guilt. Even women of choice experience some guilt about the duplicity of their involvements, although the feeling is frequently only a fleeting one. If you experience guilt, handle it:

1. Realize guilt is something you control. It comes from something you're telling yourself about the situation or what others say about you. If you truly agree with the Principles of Choice (see page 102), guilt has no space in your psyche.

2. Ask yourself, "What am I telling myself that makes the guilt justified?" Challenge the thought. If there is no basis for it, reject the thought.
3. Explore how you may be using guilt to relieve feelings of being "bad" or selfish, or to punish yourself for enjoying or accepting something that works and feels right to you.
4. If you find yourself often accepting someone else's notion of what your life should be like, *stop*. You may be feeling guilty because you're not living up to their standards of right and wrong. Don't be quick to define your life by others' mores, because lots of people are miserable doing so.

When you take full responsibility for your actions, guilt will become a thing of the past.

BIRTH CONTROL AND HEALTH PROBLEMS

It used to be that women were admonished to be chaste so that the identity of offspring would never be in question or there would be no risk of unwanted pregnancies. In the 1980's, birth control and relaxed standards of morality make these problems less traumatic. No woman has to get pregnant unless she wants to, nor does she have to see through a pregnancy unless she so chooses. The whole issue of getting pregnant, though, is still a very troublesome one for many women, especially single women with different sexual partners.

No matter how enlightened, few men take an interest in birth control. For them, it's clearly a woman's problem. In some of today's loose sexual situations, which pass for relationships, most men have little knowledge, much less interest, in what a woman must do to keep from getting pregnant. Yet, women commonly say, "I'm sick of the hassles of birth control. I can't take the Pill, and the rest of the stuff is less than foolproof. So what should I do?"

An airline stewardess named Susan, a pretty blonde, confided in me that she lived in terror of becoming pregnant. Ordered by her physician to cease using the Pill, she was forced to rely on what she felt were slipshod methods at best. "I see three different men and would have no way of even knowing who the father is if I got pregnant," she said ruefully.

It would be easy to judge her and say that that's what she gets when she fools around, but her situation is such a common one that it defies judgment. More than anything, Susan started out wanting to marry and raise a family, but she never met a man with whom she could share this goal. Not wanting to live a life without men, she worked out relationships with three men in different cities, none of whom, by the way, wanted a committed relationship. Susan's story is evidence of a point I made earlier. Women who share by choice may not always rejoice in their choice. Often it's a simple case of feeling they have limited options.

The fear of venereal and other sexually transmitted diseases is rampant in our society, and justly so. In fact, some media reports suggest that sexual promiscuity is on the decline because of people's fear of getting herpes, AIDS, and other diseases. However, women who decide to have multiple sexual partners need to be aware that they may be subjected to a variety of repeated vaginal infections, in addition to life-threatening diseases, such as AIDS. If you find yourself with more of these infections than usual, you need to consult a physician. More than that, it is perhaps time to reexamine your sexual life-style and some of your partners. According to a March of Dimes statement on sexually transmitted diseases (STD), "The risk of STD infection increases enormously in relation to the number of different people with whom a person has sexual contact. The fewer the number of contacts, the lower the risk." You must be prudent about the men you allow in your life. Try to know a little more about a man than his name before you become intimate. Of course, even having given you all the information in the world, he still may give you an infection. All you can do is exercise sound judgment, and hope that he is as interested in maintaining his health as you are.

LEARNING DISCRETION

Charting unknown waters alone can be frightening, but sharing all of the intimate details of your life with neighbors, family, and friends also can be very hazardous to your mental health. After talking with countless women in sharing situations, it seems to me best to keep the details of your relationships to yourself. Recently, I met a woman on a plane who was so excited about her trip to meet a lover that she had to share it with me. Since I didn't know her, she thought her candor was permissible. A few weeks later, at a wedding, I was introduced to a charming couple, and the wife was the lady on the plane. Needless to say, she looked faint when she saw me. I imagine she was wondering what I might say about her "secret" trip. The lesson is, keep your business to yourself. For example, if your mother constantly gives you the blues because you haven't settled down, why further aggravate your relations with her by bringing home different men each time she has you over for dinner. The same is true for office social functions. It isn't necessary to show up with a different man each time you have a work-related social engagement. If you don't want people questioning your behavior, structure your life so that you leave others out of the intimate details as much as possible.

Social functions are when having male friends becomes so important, especially for women involved in complicated intimate relations. A good buddy can fill in for you when you need an escort at particular social affairs, no one needs to know that this guy is not the love of your life. Women who are involved with married men have always had to have "public" dates, but single women can have a friend who always accompanies them to the boss's house. This is far better than having your boss quietly wonder how you keep up with your assignments, given the fact that he always sees you with a different man. Let your common sense be your guide, and don't set yourself up for trouble. A little thoughtful planning could save the day and your reputation.

COMINGS AND GOINGS

If you are single and live in an urban area, you probably live in an apartment building. This means that your comings and goings are very visible. For instance, Bill shows up Wednesday night for dinner and decides to stay the night. Your neighbor down the hall leaves the same time you do each morning and notices that on Thursday morning you have company. Lo and behold, you run into the same neighbor on Saturday, when you are coming in with Paul after an evening at the movies. The neighbor might try not to look you directly in the eyes, but rest assured that he notices that this guy is very different from the one he saw earlier in the week. No matter how tough your armor, it's easy to feel self-conscious when you know people are watching what you do. If you decide to have multiple partners, however, you must be prepared for the repercussions of a society very conflicted about morality.

When a married woman takes a lover, she must be exceedingly careful about where and how she is seen with this man. On the other hand, her husband may openly wine and dine other women under various pretenses. In fact, some single women tell me that married men are more plentiful in the so-called singles clubs than single men. One Friday evening, a tall attractive married man, whose wife had come home from the hospital that day with their new baby, told me he was out on the town seeking what he described as a "one-on-one relationship for four or five hours."

Our society permits married men to "have their needs met," especially when they moan and groan about not getting any satisfaction at home. However, who cares about all the poor women at home? When a married woman decides she, too, needs to have her needs met, she must be exceedingly careful about how she conducts her private life. Don't flaunt what you do. It can only cause problems you don't need.

MEETING THE OTHER WOMAN

A man I'll call David loaned his long-standing girl friend his car for the weekend, instructing her to keep it until Monday, because he wouldn't need it. Instead, she chose to return the car to him on Saturday, hoping to surprise him that she was actually bringing the car back early. In the meantime, a new lady love from out of town had arrived for the weekend. Having no reason to expect that his "hometown" girl would show up early with the keys, David answered the door when she knocked. His girl friend pushed her way in, having suspected all along that he had other company. The two women exchanged hostile stares, and everybody's weekend was ruined.

A married woman, irate that her husband's lover had the repeated audacity to call their home, drove to his mistress's home one evening to confront her. She threw her up against the wall and threatened "to wipe up the Pacific coast with her" if she didn't stay away from her husband. Shaken, the other woman vowed to herself that if she got out of this one, she would definitely leave this man alone.

Meeting the other woman when you least expect it can provide quite a jolt. When you are seeing someone else's guy, it's important to exercise some discretion and be ever mindful of your own protection. Women still are more apt to come after the other woman than they are to confront their erring partner. If you choose not to be a casualty, exercise some caution.

Meeting the other woman can also dispel some false illusions you may have about your lover. A woman I know who had been seeing a married man for some time became frustrated with his tentative promises about leaving his wife and decided to take matters into her own hands. She called his wife, who agreed to see her. "I don't think I can carry this lie around any longer. I want you to know that I'm involved with your husband," she told the wife. To her shock, the wife replied calmly, "Oh, you and many others." With that, the woman's knees turned to putty and, days later, she told the man she would never see him again. For her, she gleaned some very important information from meeting her lover's wife. An article in *Savvy* magazine, entitled "Love Triangles Revealed," illustrates an important point that women need to understand about the other woman. It states, "Many women come to feel a bond with their rivals, for the other woman is not only an enemy but (often) a common victim."

THE GREEN-EYED MONSTER

The women who are most unhappy about finding themselves in sharing situations may find the following tips useful in dealing with jealousy and revenge.

Jealousy is perhaps the single most hazardous component
of all sharing relationships. We all like to think of ourselves
as mature adults able to handle whatever comes our way,
but nothing can turn maturity into immaturity as quickly as
the green-eyed monster. Recognize that when someone you
care for also cares for someone else, curiosity about that
other person and jealousy may overcome you. You always
want to know how you measure up. The big question is
how to handle these discomforting feelings without letting
them handle you. Too many women immediately go on witch-
hunts for the other woman: "I'll tell her a thing or two."
The other woman, however, is not the person with whom
you have the relationship. If you feel betrayed the man owes
you some answers—not the other woman. She owes you no
explanations or reassurances, and misplaced anger spent in
her direction can tie you up in knots, wasting valuable time
that you could be using on yourself.

First, understand that jealousy is a natural emotion, even
when you knowingly are sharing a man. And when you are
unsure of your status in the relationship, you may cling more
to him. Having a shaky ego also makes you more insecure.
Your ego won't allow you to feel that any other woman can
take your place. If he adds on another woman, that's quite
a different problem than if he drops you for someone else.
Even women of choice don't like being dropped.

Look at the situation causing the jealousy and evaluate it
as objectively as you can. Is this man trying to make you
upset on purpose? Have things not been right between you

two for some time and jealousy is a mask for some general misgivings about the relationship? Ask yourself if you are a victim of the ownership monster? Do you latch on to a man so tightly that every moment he turns away from you causes feelings of loss and abandonment? Answers to these questions will help you sort out jealous emotions and put your feelings in the proper perspective.

CREATIVE REVENGE

In discussing natural emotions like love, anger, and jealousy, it would only be fair for me to mention another natural emotion—revenge. No matter how much you might want to resist the impulse to pay him back, the thoughts may occur to you, so don't be surprised. The first thought is usually to get yourself another man and try to make your man jealous. This generally backfires, because he knows that you just grabbed the first man who came along. Besides, using another guy to make your man jealous is no fun; you wind up in the arms of another, imagining yourself with the one you still love. However, if you determine that his running around is not of the serious variety and all he needs is a little nudge to pull him back in, there are a few ways to bring him home.

A friend of mine who was disgusted with her boyfriend's infidelities told me that she figured it was high time she had a little fun at his expense. She invited him over for a quiet evening, having prearranged for a dozen roses to be delivered to her the same evening. When the roses came, she oohed and aahed over them—of course, never revealing to her lover the identity of her admirer. Several days later, she sent herself some love notes, which she conveniently left around her apartment for you know who to see. When he questioned her about the notes, she gave him a knowing smile, but never any real information. Her game worked: He started cleaning up his act, and she got what she wanted—more of his devoted time and attention.

Clara, a thirty-eight-year-old divorcée, had been seeing Victor for several years and thought it was time for a commitment of some kind. The more the commitment talk increased, the antsier he got, prompting him to start becoming less available to her and more available to others. When she found out about his other sweeties, she decided he was basically a good guy in need of the right kind of nudge from a good woman. She turned her answering machine on and had her secretary screen all her calls so that he couldn't reach her at home or at work. If he came to the door, she just looked through the peephole and didn't answer. She enlisted the aid of a good friend who she knew he would call, and the friend was programmed to say she hadn't seen her around either. She kept this routine up for thirty days, and he was slowly driven mad. When she finally turned up, he demanded to know what had happened to her. Her reply was, "Oh, I just got sidetracked and have been very busy." He popped the question soon thereafter, and her disappearing days are over.

In one of her comedy routines, Joan Rivers recommends that women try what she did to pay back her husband, Edgar, for his alleged affairs. "When you think he's been out cheating," she said, "leave every toilet seat up in the house and make him think you've been cheating, too." Another woman burned down cigars in her ashtrays so that they would be conveniently noticed by an errant lover; someone else sat at McDonald's until it closed a couple of evenings and left her husband wondering where she was.

You know your man best and are in the best position to know what will work with him and what won't. The bottom line is, however, if he really doesn't care, try as hard as you might, nothing will work.

CHAPTER 10

Getting Your Act Together

Getting what you want out of life requires aligning thoughts, briefs, and intentions.
—DR. RUTH ROSS

The list of tactics found in this chapter may seem familiar to you. They are actions from earlier chapters that can get you on the road to feeling good about yourself and the men with whom you choose to relate. Consider these strategies again, just for reinforcement.

TACTIC 1 DON'T PUT HIM FIRST

Too often, when women get involved in a shared relationship, they put the needs of the man first, hoping he will give up other women. Or, women may do this in order to keep the relationship going, because they mistakenly think if a man's needs are satisfied, he will stay. The usual result, however, is that the woman is confined in a one-sided relationship that never meets her needs. You can give up everything, and he may leave anyway. When you feel that you are giving away more than you receive, take heed. You aren't getting what you deserve.

The thing to remember is that putting yourself first is not selfish. It simply means you have developed "selfness." If you're unhappy, you can't make anyone else happy. Because we are the only ones responsible for ourselves, we must ensure that our goals, needs, and desires are met.

TACTIC 2 FOLLOW YOUR INSTINCTS

Just as your instincts or intuitions can give you a clear perception of your surroundings, they can also give you an accurate reading of what is going on in your relationship, especially if you want to know if you're sharing. Don't hesitate to use your instincts or feminine intuition. They're your mechanisms for survival.

When you ignore your basic instincts about your relationship, you may feel a strong gut reaction, a sudden anxiety attack, or a sad, heavy feeling in your heart. Listen to these signals. Don't deny them. It may not be too late to make some changes in your relationship.

TACTIC 3 ACT RATHER THAN REACT

It's not uncommon for women to assume the role of peacemaker, even in a dissatisfying relationship. Because we have been conditioned to accept the man as master, leader, the one in charge, we are constantly in the position of reacting to a man's whims, his ideas, and his actions. Women often mistakenly think placating him means keeping him.

When you find yourself in an uncomfortable sharing situation, you have the option of turning that situation around to your advantage. Instead of always reacting, move forward with your own program, being reasonable, of course, but never caving in just because someone else is upset or not getting his way. Developing your own strategy will ensure that your needs are met.

TACTIC 4 DON'T GO WITH THE FLOW

Many women feel it is better to stay in a shared relationship, even if they are miserable. If you agree with this feeling, you're probably someone who "goes with the flow." The woman who goes with the flow doesn't want to challenge a partner who continuously shortchanges her, because she's afraid doing so may end the relationship.

To have a successful relationship, however, means you're willing to work to improve its shortcomings or terminate it, whatever the risks. It means you can't be afraid of making demands and negotiating around them. If things have to be his way or no way, you're better off without him. Half a loaf is half a loaf, any way you slice it.

TACTIC 5 NEVER COMMIT TO THE UNCOMMITTED

You meet a man, and the two of you start to date. Even though you know he's not the be-all and end-all, you commit yourself to the relationship. This is especially dangerous when you know this man has other women. You can enjoy his company, but don't immediately stop seeing other men yourself. You run the risk of making the relationship more than it really is. Whenever you begin a relationship, take for yourselves an appropriate grace period—perhaps three or four weeks—during which time you both explore what you want from the relationship. Then you can decide if you want to continue the relationship on whatever terms are agreeable to *both*.

Committing yourself to an uncommitted person is not wise; you could be left frustrated and disappointed.

TACTIC 6 FIND A SUPPORT SYSTEM

Always include in your life those people upon whom you can rely no matter what. For instance, my friends are constant sources of support, and not just when there's no man in my life. We need friends all of the time. Too many women drop family and friends when they meet a man. This is foolhardy, and bound to leave you in the lurch.

TACTIC 7 DON'T FEAR YOUR POWER— USE IT OR LOSE IT

You must learn to stop fearing the unknown. Decide, instead, to take control and gain the power to define yourself in spite of the "risk" of being stronger. You can't be afraid of being so self-confident that no one will be able to relate to you on an intimate basis. You may even become efficient in dealing with the social games of shared relationships: Don't take responsibility for the mistakes of men in your life. A woman who is eager to accept blame gives up her powers of negotiation. If everything is your fault, the man is off the hook and has no reason to modify his behavior. A defeatist posture is not a winning one, so push it aside. Remember, power not used ceases to be power. If you're afraid to articulate what you need and what you will and won't accept, you can't expect anyone else to figure it out. One of my favorite quotes is one from Shirley MacLaine: "If you want the fruit on the tree, you must be willing to go out on a limb."

EPILOGUE

For Each Her Own

I have come to the conclusion that whether women choose to share their men or not, they still will be subjected to the effects of man sharing. In that sense, man sharing becomes both a choice and a dilemma. If women were to get away from feeling totally responsible for upholding the moral fiber for the rest of society, there might be fewer feelings of conflict. However, whatever a woman's ultimate decision, there are a host of other accompanying choices and concerns. Sharing doesn't become less troublesome because you agree or disagree with it.

Sharing is not a new social situation. Men and women have always had affairs for a variety of reasons, which I've discussed. Today, factors like the male shortage, fear of commitment, and rapid change of social roles for men and women have thrown us into an atmosphere very conducive to sharing. Unfortunately, wherever you stand on the issue—right or wrong—the reality is that you can't avoid it. As a woman, I understand and sympathize with the cruelty of having to cope with a reality that I didn't choose, but as I have indicated throughout this book, the only person in control of your life is *you*. With that thought in mind, I never tell women what they should do, nor do I urge them to adopt a life-style they can't handle.

I began this book wondering how women could make life work on their own terms, even while facing disappointments, hurts, and tremendous risks. The answer is that women must learn how to embrace life and live it with courage and a great sense of their own power. I've learned this, and the truth that what life becomes is what you make it. In an interesting way, at every turning point, we're just learning that we're offered the opportunity to clear up our mistakes and establish new options. The irony is that that choice has always been ours to make. In relationships, we often end up with whatever we're willing to settle with. If you want monogamous relationships, you may end up taking a stance by accepting only what you feel you can consciously live with.

With the women I advise, I undertake a mirroring process so that they can review, based upon their own experiences and philosophies, who they are and what it is they will have to do to get what they need out of this life. For most women, single and married the issue of sharing a man is a traumatic situation. However, the alternatives to sharing, which for singles can often mean being alone and bitter or constantly chasing fantasies, can be just as traumatic emotionally.

I understand and sympathize with the frustrations of women brought up to believe that monogamy is the only acceptable life-style, only to discover as adults a much different reality. When women ask me, "How can I live a meaningful life without a mate?" I tell them that they can have men in their lives, but perhaps not in the traditional ways they had expected. They may have to share for brief periods, or in the long term with the same group of people, or may even eventually choose to drop out. If women continue to believe that there is only one way to relate to the opposite sex, the frustrations we see now in social relations will only continue.

As I have indicated throughout this book, there always are alternatives for any woman who chooses to explore them.

My hope for women is that more will adopt an attitude of "for each her own," becoming as comfortable asserting themselves in their private lives as some have become in their professional lives. Taking responsibility for one's self isn't easy, but it's necessary for women in order to reduce their feelings of resentment and helplessness in relationships. They must strive toward self-empowerment, making wise choices that are based on what's real. They must develop a healthier way to connect with men, embracing the fact that men and women are both dependent and independent people. When they do this, they will reduce the probability of conflict in their relationships.

It pains me to see women who have worked so hard to build professional competence come completely unglued at the antics of the men in their lives. They seem to spend less time on sexual politics and more on social activities. This doesn't prepare you for how to deal with today's sharing dynamics. I hasten to add that self-empowerment should never be confused with the egotistical self-absorption so rampant in current male-female relations.

We are deeply embroiled in a social limbo that is confusing to both men and women who seek intimate connections beyond the purely sexual. Many still use emotional flight and superficial jargon as protection from involvement. Few of us can admit needing someone, because the vulnerability that goes with it is too scary. Consequently, countless adults struggle with the anxiety and frustration of aloneness, yet they are too afraid to step from behind the walls they have erected around themselves. To be sure, avoiding intimacy and its concomitant responsibilities will enable you to abate feelings of pain and disappointment. The result, however, is a "safe" life on the middle ground of emotional territory with no lows but certainly no highs either.

Every living creature survives through some aspect of bonding. It's a basic human need to desire touching, affection, and care, whether you are an infant or a senior citizen. This desire for connection and intimacy will never change; why we think we can make it alone defies my comprehension. For this reason, I hope that in the future married people will strive harder to seek solutions to their problems within the marriage. In this book, I have described a society where sharing flourishes among both singles and marrieds, but clearly the practice can have deleterious effects on the future of family life in this country. I guess the question is how we can find our way back to trusting enough to allow intimate connection. Trust is just one side of the picture; being a responsible person is the other equally significant side.

Both men and women are responsible for conditions in today's relationships, so both will need to join together to create constructive connections. Values and ethics have been challenged in the past few years, yet sexual health problems and the lack of closeness and intimacy are causing many people to reconsider the old ways. Even though these ways weren't perfect, they may do more to encourage relationships of substance. This may mean that even if the male shortage continues, there will be less casual sex and more committed sharing with longevity. Friendship will become more important as the base for establishing love.

Women must take some of the blame for the mess we find ourselves in today with men. Some women have taken things too far in relationships, having made themselves too available with few chances for getting what they want. Now, most have found that what they need is also some assurance of stability in their relationships. Women struck out on a course to free ourselves without ever involving the men. No wonder, then, that many males harbor deep resentments and quietly say among themselves, "They wanted freedom, well now they have it. Let's see how they like it." Some men have taken this attitude and made it an easy excuse for treating women in as shabby a fashion as they choose. While there are many men who have no desire to mistreat women, they inadvertently do so out of sheer confusion as to what their proper role should be.

As Betty Friedan said, "Our past error was promoting a social movement for the liberation of women without realizing that what's at stake is really human liberation." If women want freedom from the stringent roles of yesteryear, we must recognize that men also need some relief from the worn-out roles they have been forced to play.

Once you accept that autonomy and responsibility are not mutually exclusive in any life, then you can be relieved of having to carry alone the burdens of an antiquated morality that few people adhere to anyway. I urge you to realize that life continually offers choices that often come with consequences you don't always desire. With this thought in mind, I strongly suggest you seek personal fulfillment based upon your own values and needs, not someone else's. This means learning how to take care of yourself, but most of all, it means learning to respect and love yourself.

Bibliography

Abeel, Erica. *I'll Call You Tomorrow.* New York: William Morrow, 1981.

Cassell, Carol. *Swept Away.* New York: Simon & Schuster, 1984.

Chesler, Phyllis, and Emily J. Goodman. *Women, Money, and Power.* New York: William Morrow, 1978.

Dowling, Collette. *The Cinderella Complex.* New York: Summit Books, 1981.

Ehrenreich, Barbara. *The Hearts of Men.* New York: Anchor Press-Doubleday, 1983.

Gilligan, Carol. *In a Different Voice.* Cambridge, Mass.: Harvard University Press, 1982.

Goldberg, Herb. *The New Male.* New York: William Morrow, 1979.

———. *The Hazard of Being Male.* New York: New American Library, 1976.

Guttenberg, Marcia, and Paul F. Secord. *Too Many Women.* Beverly Hills: Sage Publications, 1982.

Kernberg, Otto. *Borderline Conditions and Pathological Narcissisms.* New York: Jason Aronson, 1975.

Lasch, Christopher. *The Culture of Narcissism.* New York: W. W. Norton, 1979.

Miller, Jean Baker. *Toward a New Psychology of Women.* Boston: Beacon Press, 1975.

Naifeh, Steven, and Gregory White Smith. *Why Can't Men Open Up?* New York: Clarkson N. Potter, 1984.

BIBLIOGRAPHY

Novak, William. *The Great American Male Shortage and Other Roadblocks to Romance.* New York: Rawson, 1983.

Sands, Melissa. *Survival Guide for the Mistress.* New York: Berkley Publishing, 1978.

Staples, Robert. *The World of Black Singles.* Westport, Conn.: Greenwood Press, 1981.

Schnall, Maxine. *A Search for New Values.* New York: Clarkson N. Potter, 1981.

Toffler, Alvin. *Future Shock.* New York: Random House, 1970.

West, Uta. *Women in a Changing World.* New York: McGraw-Hill, 1975.

————. *If Love Is the Answer, What Is the Question?* New York: McGraw-Hill, 1977.

Wolfe, Linda. *The Cosmo Report: Women and Sex in the 80's.* New York: Bantam Books, 1981.